Automotive Alchemy In India

By Sanmit Prabhat Akhilesh Dixit

Powered by

Mekit.in

The Automotive Alchemy In India.

Copyright © 2024 Sanmit Dixit.

All rights reserved.

Book cover designed by Sanmit Dixit.

For Dadu, Dadi, Dad & my AAI

Contents

Author's preface

Whenever we pick up a customer's car for any work, we take loads of photos of the car's condition and check all electronics & functions forming a pickup report. Irony is that I have been making the inventory report since I was 16. That's when I learned to drive, sneaking out almost every night, very well planned & executed (parents could never figure out in 300+ attempts). I would click 50+ pictures, place a marker object on the front side of the tires so that I could park it exactly how it was. That meant keeping everything precise - fuel level, gear, AC speed, seat height, you name it.

Then, one day, my parents left me home alone for an event, and could mean only one thing - time to take friends for a drive, but this time during the day. They were supposed to be back by 8 pm, so I had it all planned to be home by 7 pm. On my way back, my car broke down just 25 minutes away from home. Nobody knew what to do, whom to call for help, and I was scared of only one thing, what if my parents reach before me. So I called one of my friends who insisted on getting a jumpstart upon arriving and he was absolutely right. The car then started and thanks to Shreyash, I reached home before my parents. That day, stuck on the road and feeling lost, I quickly opened the notes app and wrote "Remote mechanic for vehicles. I mean call for anything for vehicles anywhere" in a note labelled "Uncensored ideas." I would regularly note down ideas that I thought had some potential or were design wise too faulty without any thought of pursuing it.

Fast forward to today, I run Mekit with a vision to revolutionise the automotive ecosystem starting with garage interactions, a space where all our predecessors have failed in the race to "digitise" the industry by building a technological wall (app) between the vehicle owner and the garage and simply take a cut off that intro after spending lot to get eyeballs on the app. We had a strong hypothesis that if we instead can organise each car responsibility through a trusted expert, without charging any commissions or fees from any party, at your preferred vendor (dealership or third party), then we might end up playing a major role in the relationship between a car owner and a car. Getting to this hypothesis involved quite a journey with its fair share of twists, turns, and adventures, in fact it started with solving for the breakdown experience. I'll save that story for another post, but taking this different route exposed us to a lot of market and industry insights, especially since we work at dealerships as well as third party vendors, we had the luxury of observing and learning from both sides of the court. Surprisingly, what we initially considered standard industry knowledge turned out to be misconceptions, contrary even to the beliefs of industry experts and also in large context supports why most previous autocare startups haven't been able to Mekit big (pun intended) or failed.

So over the years, I became an avid note taker and now whenever I observe something or come across a thought, whether or not it can be turned into an insight later, I instantly pick my phone and start typing. Now that includes anything from a feedback session with a user, todos, observations, just random ideas, personal feelings. You might have guessed that when I mentioned being an 'avid' note taker. Every few months, I'd try to organise these drafts using different apps, but I never quite succeeded. However, among the chaos, I stumbled upon many drafts that amazed me. You know that feeling when you come across some insight you'd like to bookmark forever? Well, these were like those, but in the world of automotive. So, this write-up is a detailed dive into several of my 2500+ drafts from the last 2 years since I began working on Mekit, including some longer pieces that were kept just for myself or the team.

I don't know if I have achieved the right to write this book, but if it manages to quench the curiosity of even one person then I guess my 60 hours that went into writing this book will be totally worth it. I also figured it will continue to serve as a repository of insights for me and the team. So fasten your seatbelts, I hope you have a fantastic ride...err I mean, read.

1G to 5G

The first generation of wireless communication, 1G, was launched in 1979, a time when both cars and phones were luxuries meant only for the wealthy. Roads were less crowded, and car repair shops were scarce. This scarcity meant that almost every car owner needed to maintain a good relationship with their garage owner. Why? Because warranty periods lasted only a year, and getting parts replaced under warranty often depended on your rapport with the garage. Sounds unbelievable, right? Some car owners even sent Diwali gifts to their mechanics to keep the relationship strong. Plus, complaining wasn't as easy as clicking a button on the internet back then.

Back then, repairing your car was a lengthy process, often requiring you to spend days at the workshop alongside the mechanic, making sure everything was happening in front of your eyes. This was crucial since a car was more than just transportation; it was a valued possession, and remote communication wasn't as effective. You didn't understand the technical stuff, so you had no choice but to trust the mechanic. Ordering and getting parts was also slow, and "jugaad" was very common at every level.

People even then were ready to pay extra to get a car delivered earlier, and buying a new car was no less than a ceremony where people would start by thanking the almighty, following rituals like putting up a Swastik or Nimbu mirchi in case of Hindus, and every new car purchase also meant a day spent at the accessories shop: sunfilm, front crash guard, guards for the side, rear indicators, stereo, seat covers, and if you were in the mood to spend, wheel rims, side mouldings, and whatnot.

There were very few fuel stations, so you always had to carry paper maps and sometimes ask strangers to confirm the direction. There were no food courts, ATMs, or roadside assistance, and every breakdown was a horrible experience. The Mumbai-Pune road used to be a famous point for clutch burns, with 60 kmph being fast. Those were quite different times! Today, we've got garages almost everywhere, mobile phones, Google Maps, ATMs, roadside help, and plenty of restaurants across most of the country, and the spirit of jugaad still persists. For example, look at this recent photo I clicked at a garage. The mechanic used a cardboard piece to fix a rattling noise from the front bumper.

In fact, we've come a long way from 1G to now having 5G in the last five decades. But you know what's interesting? The core experience of owning a vehicle and handling its responsibilities is still the same: unorganised, time-consuming, offline, non-transparent, and whatnot. It's pretty surprising, considering it's the common man's second biggest purchase after a house. Let me share something fascinating. Remember how the Mumbai-Pune highway was notorious for clutch plate burns? Check this out: the below photo isn't from the 1980s; it's from December 25th, 2023, with several cars on the road showing clutch plate burns on that same famous highway.

Over 100 clutch plates die in ghat traffic on way to Pune

Umesh K Parida / TNN / Updated: Dec 26, 2023, 11:19 IST   135 PTS   SHARE   AA   FOLLOW US

Courtesy: The Times Of India

Every car essentially involves three types of work. First, there's what I call 'beauty parlour' work, which covers all cosmetic aspects like denting and painting, detailing, accessories, modifications, cleaning, etc. The second category is surgery, which includes repairs and replacements of parts and electronics as well as periodic servicing. Finally, there's the miscellaneous category, covering everything else - from insurance and PUC renewal to tires, fastag, RTO work, towing, battery-related tasks, you name it. These categories resonate with most people because they mirror real-life scenarios. For instance, consider someone leaving the hospital after a major surgery and then visiting a salon to get their hair dyed. The most noticeable change to friends would likely be the new hair colour. Similarly, the beauty parlour work gets noticed first, and this minor work plays a critical role in shaping a customer's perception. If these smaller tasks aren't completed, doubts arise about the completion of major repairs. Additionally, beauty parlour jobs are quickly rated, unlike surgery work, which lacks immediate feedback. Car owners have limited ways to assess it beyond driving experience changes, particularly absent in work done as a part of preventive measures. This delayed feedback, lack of understanding, and other factors that we will talk about later in the book contribute to a very low Net Promoter Score (NPS) in the autocare industry. It is immensely difficult to crack that, and as per me, there isn't anyone who has been able to solve this at scale, including some mass market dealerships.

While family members delve deep into understanding a patient's illness, the same level of understanding isn't present in the automotive context. There's often no drive to grasp the intricacies behind car parts and their functionality. Even if someone wants to, the service advisors lack comprehensive training, so it will unnecessarily sound very complicated without much clarity, and the mechanics struggle to effectively communicate these details. Every repair is so personalised to you that looking for the problem online will almost always not give you a direction unless you are geeky enough to dive into niche communities like

TeamBHP that facilitate this level of knowledge sharing. Thank you, and much love to the folks there.

This gap in communication often leads to a lingering concern that they might be deceived or overcharged - for instance, just cleaning the filter and putting it back while charging for a replacement. This kind of suspicion is one of the reasons that prompts people to stand with their cars throughout the entire service. Unfortunately, automotive is one of the industries that still lacks instant access to shared knowledge accessible to millions. This situation rings a bell about the jewellery market before Caratlane disrupted the industry by bringing it online. In the past, when customers entered a shop, their options were limited to what the shopkeeper had on display. This restricted access meant that what the shopkeeper presented was the primary source for understanding market trends and design options. One notable difference between automotive and healthcare is that, in healthcare, incidents are always unfortunate and not universally experienced by each individual. Conversely, in automotive, an internal combustion engine (ICE) boasts extensive data on common issues at specific mileage and age intervals. This familiarity allows some individuals, especially those who've owned new cars before, to anticipate forthcoming expenses, offering more predictability and a lot more potential to significantly improve NPS across the industry. You might notice that I've directed most of my statements towards males rather than maintaining gender neutrality. This is due to the significantly lower representation of females engaged in both driving and maintaining their cars.

In all these years, there were many companies that entered the automotive scene, some introducing completely new business types with lots of innovation, while others chose to pick a niche task out of the above three categories and optimise existing methods at scale.

Among these entrants are facilitators in used car transactions such as Cars24, CarTrade, Droom, Spinny, etc. as well as parking assistance platforms like Park+ and Parkmate. Additionally, there's a range of self-driving car rental services, including Zoomcar, Carzonrent, and Revv, providing convenient options for users. Car-information portals like CarInfo and CarWho have also emerged. Moreover, the industry now boasts car leasing firms like PumPumPum, mobility solutions like Ola and Yulu, and spare parts suppliers such as Boodmo. Furthermore, companies like Zekardo have ventured into the pre-delivery inspection of new cars, while entities like Loconav specialise in fleet management solutions. Notably, media platforms like Autocar and Rushlane, along with insurance providers such as Acko and InsuranceDekho, have also made their mark in the industry. There are also entities like DriveU, which provides drivers on demand; on-board diagnostics services like Scouto; and tire marketplaces such as

Tyreplex. Additionally, financial services like Rupyy, which offers car loans, and ReadyAssist, which promises reliable roadside assistance on subscription, have entered the scene. Another noteworthy category that has emerged in the last 5–10 years is the "creators," who play a significant role in the ecosystem. Names like Autocar, HorsepowerCartel, Faisal Khan, MotorOctane, Motorbeam, Powerdrift, NamasteCar, Ask CarGuru, MyCarHelpline, and others have leveraged their influence for various offerings, including new car purchase consultancy, merchandise, events, races, new car launches, and much more.

It's fascinating how the automotive industry operates on such an intricate scale, with countless components needing synchronisation for a seamless drive. This complexity has spurred the growth of auto-tech startups, leveraging innovation in this space.

There is one more category that I believe has a very low degree of PMF in the Indian market: the tech-enabled car maintenance companies like GoMechanic, Carpathy, Carmozo, Gobumpr, Pitstop, Carnation, and others. In this book, I will thoroughly explore this particular category, covering all the roles and journeys in great detail. The vast array of components also signifies a multitude of vendors catering to multiple companies. In fact, the automotive industry directly and indirectly employs around 19 million individuals and contributes significantly to our nation's GDP, accounting for 7.1%.

As we advanced from 1G to using 5G today, the automotive sector also touched massive scale. For instance, the monthly registration of passenger cars in 2023 is ten times the number of cars built in India back in 1980 (3,00,000: 30,487). Furthermore, a significant share of cars in India are owned by the top 7.5% of households. Interestingly, despite the booming startup culture, these auto-tech companies hold a relatively smaller market share. The industry predominantly operates offline, showcasing the substantial presence of numerous entities: garages, parts suppliers, tire and battery vendors, insurance providers, manufacturing units, dealerships, logistics, value-added service providers, and many more, all collectively shaping the automotive landscape.

Let me walk you through what it's like for someone in India to buy a car. Imagine you've been doing well at work, getting promotions and bonuses, and you've recently sold an old property, making some good money. You decide it's time to act on your plan and get yourself a car. You start by browsing the internet and test-driving a few models. Here's a tip: don't judge the after-sales service based on how friendly they are while selling; sometimes, they'll do everything to persuade you to buy. After trying out three cars, you might go online to find every tiny detail about the car you prefer. The salespeople follow up at least seven times after your test drive - 21 calls in the next few weeks! The sales boss insists on selling extended warranties and insurance because it's extra profit for the dealership and accessories are a big deal; you can bargain on those for a cash discount. After negotiating on insurance and accessories, you make the purchase. Some individuals opt to save by getting accessories from third-party vendors, seemingly a bargaining tactic that often ends up being the brand's price. With a new car, you enjoy a warranty of 100,000 kilometres or three years, along with the first three services, labour-free. However, this warranty process isn't as straightforward as it seems, and I'll delve deeper into this in the chapter dedicated to dealerships.

Fun fact: a lot of people who own high-end cars (anything above ₹1 crore) sell them away and buy a new car every 5 years. This is because they purchase the car along with a very intensive maintenance package that covers most things, including wear and tear parts required within a span of 5 years, along with an extended warranty for any manufacturer faults during that period. This is further backed up by all-inclusive insurance, ensuring they are protected from major expenses unless the repair amount exceeds 50% of the IDV. So, after the 5th year, many of these owners sell the car, as there is a lot of liability associated with car ownership once the warranty and insurance have significantly lower IDVs and the maintenance package has expired. Consequently, they instantly buy a new car equipped with the same packages.

Now, let's talk about the AMC (Annual Maintenance Contract), a goldmine for dealerships, exclusively available at their workshops. This guarantees customer retention for them. Interestingly, a few individuals from the start despise dealerships, considering them scam workshops. They disregard the warranty and prefer third-party garages instead. Upon receiving the car, a small group invests more to safeguard the paint quality long-term, opting for ceramic or PPF coating, ranging from an average of ₹20,000 for the former to around a lakh for the latter across various car types. Some people do not get any of this done until the first service, when they are offered a package by the dealership including Teflon coating, anti-rust coating, and engine bay coating for approximately ₹10,000, prompting another small group to opt for this deal. After purchasing the car, it's compulsory to arrange insurance before driving it off the showroom, along with RTO charges, accessories, and external coatings as primary 'expected' expenses in the first year. It's crucial to emphasise the term 'expected,' significantly altering its meaning. More cars on the road often means more brand-specific dealerships across the country. However, accessibility remains a challenge for many, requiring a visit to the dealership and dedicating an entire day even for minor, 5-minute tasks due to queued cars, so some individuals rely on trusted third-party garages for minor jobs, maintaining a good rapport established with their previous cars, and these jobs almost always never interfere with warranty, more like the ones that can be done by yourself with help from Youtube.

Conversely, certain individuals persist in visiting only the dealership, regardless of time or money spent, a behaviour sustained until they sell the car. Subsequently, a larger group transitions to third-party workshops after the warranty expires, highlighting how an extended warranty subtly acts as a retention strategy for dealerships. Post-warranty, car owners are divided into three categories: those preferring dealerships, those preferring third-party workshops, and those without a preference, likely avoiding dealerships.

Vehicle maintenance behaviors vary widely, considering factors like timelines, budgets, and more. I would like to introduce an additional layer of categorization to signify varying attitudes toward vehicle upkeep: crypto, intraday, mutual fund, and FD. Until the warranty and insurance cover everything, the car usually remains in good condition. However, after that, some individuals drive the car until a problem surfaces. They prioritise cosmetic upgrades over crucial mechanical repairs—I term this the 'crypto set,' taking risks without guaranteed rewards. Others take some risks but strive to maintain a logical approach. They delay repair schedules, such as servicing the car after 16–18 months instead of the recommended 12 or replacing tires after 6 years instead of 4. They only undertake necessary repairs to ensure smooth driving - these are the 'Intraday people' in my categorization. Please don't take offence; these terms explain risk capacity.

Then there are individuals who tend to handle necessary car maintenance but also smartly save money whenever possible. They don't blindly rely on dealerships and usually make informed decisions about their car purchases. They might not replace tires precisely on time and might not delve much into regular car detailing, but they aim to maintain their car in good condition - a standard you or I might consider acceptable, these are what I would call "Mutual fund" set

Finally, there are passionate car owners. They prefer keeping their car in pristine condition at all times, ready to spend on relevant accessories, mostly frequent dealerships, and ensuring comprehensive maintenance, regardless of their average monthly car usage, and I call them the FD group. For the previous three categories, spending on a car largely depends on its usage. They often delay significant expenses until a breakdown occurs, justifying it with 'arey gaadi toh chalti hi nahi hai, badme karlenge.' The irony is that a car used infrequently might end up becoming more costly in the long run. Among these groups, the most discount-conscious individuals, consistently seeking 'jugaad,' follow a pattern from the highest count in the crypto category, gradually decreasing through the intraday, mutual fund, and finally the FD categories. In the initial three years, a car owner covering approximately 1000 kilometres per month typically incurs expenses for several necessities. These include annual renewal costs for first-party insurance, as third-party insurance is commonly obtained for three to five years at the point of purchase. Additionally, regular expenses involve yearly periodic service that includes oil changes, replacement of oil, AC and air filters, wheel alignment and balancing, Fastag expenses, three renewals for Pollution Under Control (PUC) certificates, and some unforeseen minor repairs especially denting & painting. It's anticipated that major repairs are often covered within the insurance or warranty terms during this period. Interestingly enough, wheel balancing and rotation seem to be largely ignored by many. It's almost as if nobody cares about the tires, yet they're actually one of the most neglected aspects of vehicle maintenance, but in reality, this negligence is quite critical. Driving less can lead to quicker tire wear, with cracks appearing in as little as 7-8 months. But I have noticed that when you explain what wheel balancing and alignment mean in easy terms, people start to understand and want to get it done. I've even seen some folks who, after realising its importance, start telling others about it. Let me break it down for you. Driving a car inherently involves uneven forces; the roads, potholes, speed breakers, turning angles, parking manoeuvres, and braking all contribute to this imbalance. These variations exert uneven pressure on the tires, causing uneven wear. For instance, during a sudden brake, only a specific portion of the tire takes the impact. Wheel balancing involves measuring these imbalances. The machine reveals areas with less impact, represented by negative grams (contrasted with the opposite side, where there's no impact, thus registered as 0 grams). To rectify this, weights are added to balance out the wear and make it 0 grams. Another factor is that many mass-market cars in India are front-wheel drive, leading to the front tires being primarily engaged in braking and wearing out faster. Hence, rotating the tires every 5000 km is recommended – swapping the front tires with the back, ensuring even wear across all tires. Now, look at this photo and compare it with what you just learnt.

It is often a leap of faith when a service provider suggests a car repair. Since there is nothing a layman car owner can do to verify the suggestion, you will often see them asking, "Pakka karwana chahiye?" (Should I really get it done?). But here's the catch: the answer to this question almost always tends to be biased. Saying "yes"

often means more profit for them, and truthfully, it doesn't always make a significant difference for you. Sure, there are a few good folks out there (bless them), but this scenario represents the majority of the market. Contrary to, let's say, the clothing e-commerce scene, where people can browse trends and designs effortlessly, the automotive market lacks this transparency. You will hardly see anyone asking the mechanic to follow something they saw or read online. Instead, they usually approve all the jobs, and one subtle reason behind this approval lingers in their minds. They want to ensure no breakdowns happen when travelling with their family, almost like buying a ticket to avoid a breakdown on the way. There are also a few people who call one of their friends and ask them if they are being fooled and what can be skipped from the estimate. This pattern echoes the past, resembling Maintenance 1.0. Today, I see it evolving into phase 3.0 while dealerships have begun online appointment bookings and service history, and a few third-party garage aggregators have emerged (although some have already dried up and we will talk about that later), the fundamental experience remains largely offline and still a task that people take an office leave for, leading to a very unorganised arrangement with a very low NPS. People also in the back of their minds always feel that they are being taken for a ride; for a matter of fact, if you look at any third-party workshop, most of them do not send service reminders, no follow-ups, no updates or reports. Cars are delivered late, and minor cosmetic fixes may get overlooked, which actually matters a lot to consumers. Despite all this, these workshops retain their customers, relying heavily on this loyalty as they don't actively market themselves. Could it be that people have simply gotten used to this subpar service?

Playground

The phrase 'Data is the new oil' has echoed across industries, resonating the profound value data holds. But here's the thing: despite significant technological advancements over the past few decades and a widespread understanding of the pivotal role data plays, the automotive sector in India remains severely starved of comprehensive data infrastructure. So, even with all the cool tech we have now, when it comes to cars, we mostly know just how many cars were sold last month, and that's been the same for ages. This limited scope has persisted unchanged, leaving industry stakeholders grappling with generalized assumptions about their customers and treating everyone the same. They sort of assume the worst about everyone, just in case someone's trying to deceive them, unfortunately penalising a significant majority of responsible car owners, relegating them to the same treatment as those engaging in wrong practices. Moreover, the barely sufficient data available, other than the monthly unit sales, especially on the customer end, represents just one aspect of the entire picture. This data is often curated by industry giants, which tend to lose touch with ground realities outside the dealerships that control a significant market share. In my previous chapter, I had to introduce multiple categories of car owners just to provide a glimpse into user types. While some startups might have published data, it's crucial to acknowledge potential biases. Their limited knowledge stems from not fully understanding a user's experience within dealerships or third-party garages because their market is totally different and cannot be generalised. The sheer vastness of the market, coupled with its unorganised and offline infrastructure, contributes to this gap. This case of data bias has been different for me at Mekit. Since the time we launched our operations, all the learning and the drafts that led me to write this book have been derived from touching every side of the market, and we are probably the only ones to do so because we work across the spectrum, including dealerships, third-party workshops, roadside garages, all third-party vendors, technology-savvy users, and even those using 'outdated' button phones. This extensive interaction has provided us with invaluable data leverage, enabling us to confidently claim a comprehensive understanding of every side of the coin. Indeed, just like the market, the user base is incredibly diverse. Consider the user base of Zerodha and Zomato – tech-savvy, English-speaking individuals frequently valuing convenience as much as cashback and attracted to various means of engagement. These platforms transformed offline services into online realms, amplifying efficiency tenfold. However, in the auto maintenance industry, despite its predominantly offline nature, the concept of transitioning online remains far from mainstream. Coupled with insufficient education and delays in various aspects, the user base feels distanced from the digital landscape.

The most significant delay factor for third-party workshops, impacting the car owner, is the availability, pricing, and authenticity of spare parts. Managing a comprehensive spare parts inventory at scale, necessitating a warehouse, is exceedingly challenging, especially when it comes to cataloguing. An organised approach to this could greatly benefit everyone involved. Currently, the spare parts industry for third-party workshops operates heavily on jugaad solutions.

This situation is directly linked to manufacturers' desire to control every car's maintenance journey through their dealerships. Manufacturers heavily prioritise spare part allocation, with the bulk designated for new car manufacturing, followed by after-sales repair parts for dealerships and warranty coverage. The least allocated is typically reserved for the third-party market.

With the exception of Tata and Maruti Suzuki, sourcing parts from other companies is becoming increasingly difficult.

For each part, there's an option to buy a used one at a significantly lower cost from nearby markets. These parts are usually taken out of vehicles intended for scrapping or sold to salvage buyers by insurance companies in cases of total vehicle loss. They're then individually sold at varied prices, often influenced by part availability. In some instances, you might be quoted twice the price of a used part compared to the cost of a new, original one. Some markets, such as Kurla in Mumbai, specialise in these parts. If there were a capital for automotive in India, let alone spare parts, it would be none other than Delhi. It stands out as a hub for everything, even parts that are not found in other regions. Many value-added cosmetic shops also prefer sourcing goods from Delhi due to the numerous manufacturing units present there. The automotive spares market remains highly unorganised, so unorganised that Mr. Jagdish Khattar, who founded Carnation, a multibrand workshop startup, after his tenure at Maruti Suzuki as its MD, later chose to shut it down, and I think it was mainly due to the unpredictable and dominating nature of the spare parts market. Like in the case of a third-party garage, where I mentioned spare parts are the biggest laggards, the garage owner has to make quite a few calls to arrange for a part for a customer with a type of car that is known to have inadequate parts supply in the market. The frequency of such cars in garages is low, and hence they can do some jugaad, put in efforts, and arrange the part from somewhere, even if it is from a place like Kurla. However, the downside here is that jugaad, as a solution, lacks scalability.

Data holds immense potential for everyone in the automotive industry. Currently, only dealerships send reminders, typically around the 11-month mark, banking on the hope that the customer will agree during the 12-month follow-ups. A significant advantage in the automotive world is the ability to predict a car's consumption pattern, which leads to every outreach being content to the end user instead of spam. The prime difference between both is "relevance." By simply asking about average monthly driving and comparing it with the odometer reading whenever the car arrives in the workshop, dealerships could send precise reminders when they're truly needed. For instance, someone driving 2000 km per month might require service every five months, making any reminder sent beyond that time wasteful. If such a person is dependent on the service centre for the service reminder, then God bless them. In that case, scheduled replacements of parts like spark plugs, which might not significantly impact the driver's experience but are crucial as per manufacturer recommendations, often get delayed or overlooked. A replacement suggested at 30,000 km might never occur on time because drivers aren't usually aware of these replacements, let alone make specific workshop visits solely for this purpose. Some dealerships even opt to prepone without valid reasons, bombarding customers with reminders multiple months in advance, akin to a mobile phone recharge model. Just like a 28-day recharge pack leads to 13 phone network recharges in a year, advancing even one service appointment earns them extra service from the customer, increasing their profits.

Every car operates uniquely in its own environment, which leads to varied maintenance needs. Dealerships can make use of this understanding and track individual requirements, not just for essential repairs but also for cosmetic touch-ups on every car whenever it arrives in the workshop. This data can be easily used to predict potential issues at certain intervals personalised to each car and send reminders at the right time, along with a rough estimation of the job in picture.

People often have the perception that dealerships are very expensive, so this proactive approach allows them to have pricing estimates handy on their phones as a comparative reference when seeking estimates from third-party workshops. For example, the labour charges for a Ford Freestyle at the dealership are low, so it would not make sense if a person were to go to a third-party workshop only for an economical difference. So here, a person will never try to find out these rates, as the perceived notion might be that dealerships are excessively expensive.

Workshops have a significant advantage: each car is due for a periodic service every 12 months, which means a guaranteed visit every 12 months. During these visits, workshops not only attend to the scheduled service but also identify and address additional issues, generating more revenue. Customers, on the other hand, mentally categorise car issues into visits: urgent breakdowns, major inconveniences, and minor pending tasks. Urgent breakdowns demand immediate attention, as they affect the car's functionality. Major or minor expenses causing significant inconvenience are scheduled based on user convenience and may face delays. Meanwhile, smaller tasks are often postponed until the next scheduled service.

Another good example that I would like to share of where data can play a pivotal role is insurance. Today, insurers often deny zero-depreciation add-ons for older vehicles due to perceived wear-and-tear risks. However, comprehensive data on user behaviour, maintenance history, and major repairs through a physical inspection of the car could potentially enable insurers to offer the zero depreciation add-on to worthy people with good behaviour towards their old car, thus increasing revenue and ultimately customer satisfaction. Furthermore, educating customers about insurance limitations and procedures is crucial. Many claim minor damages, like a small scratch, assuming all damages, old and new, will be covered. However, such claims for pre-existing damages are typically rejected. Educating customers about these limitations can prevent such scenarios, reduce unnecessary claims, and foster a clearer understanding of insurance processes. This not only reduces frustrations for customers but also enhances brand reputation by ensuring customers are well-informed about the coverage details. Understanding insurance costs can be tricky. For instance, if your policy costs ₹26,000 and includes a 25% No Claim Bonus (NCB) deduction of ₹6,500 due to no claims in the previous tenure, claiming for any job worth up to ₹7,500 wouldn't bring much advantage. That's because it would result in losing the NCB worth ₹6,500 in the next renewal, along with paying a compulsory deductible of ₹1,000, making the overall monetary benefit zero. Additionally, insurance policy pricing isn't straightforward. Losing the NCB affects the overall policy discounting, and diesel cars often face higher rates in such cases compared to petrol cars. So, despite the perception of gaining from a claim, the reality might lead to higher costs in the subsequent policy renewal.

I have seen dealerships often push for claims, even for minor repairs. For instance, if your left tail light breaks and needs replacement for about ₹3,500 with additional labour charges of around ₹500 + GST, totaling roughly ₹4,090, and you get the car back the same day or the next day, the dealership might suggest more extensive repairs. They could claim that the panel alignment where the tail light fits is bent and needs fixing. Moreover, they might propose replacing the bumper and repairing an older dent on the quarter panel, issues you might have overlooked before. This bundled offer might seem appealing; after all, who doesn't appreciate some free repairs? You might find it tempting, especially if you were hesitant about paying for just the tail lamp, so you happily agreed to claim the insurance. The repairs progress, and an advisor informs you that the new tail light is fitted, the bumper is painted, and the quarter panel work is completed. They also mention that they didn't need to do any additional work on the alignment issue. You're thrilled that the work is done and anticipate getting the car back by just paying ₹1,000 for the compulsory deductible. However, the dealership bills the insurance company for not just the actual repair but also for the panel work they claimed to have done. What should have been an expense of around ₹4,000 now balloons to a bill of ₹25,000. Despite getting your car back in ten days, this inflated bill impacts your next insurance renewal negatively. This is a classic example of how estimates can soar unexpectedly at any garage or dealership. Customers often lack the awareness or interest to grasp these complexities; anything beyond their current knowledge seems like a headache they'd rather avoid. A simple understanding of when to claim could significantly benefit you and, particularly, the insurance company. I could go on and on about how developing data in the automobile business may genuinely unlock much more potential for growth in all sectors. Another example is that many of the startups that have emerged in the last few years specifically for car maintenance only work with third-party workshops; however, I feel there is a lot more that can be unlocked from enormous garage data. One can determine who specialises in what, what is the behaviour, particularly cheating, how well the diagnostics, punctuality, ethics, and so much more can be beautifully integrated into the master system, benefiting all the parts and thus attempting to slightly improve the way the garages function and organise some areas for them.

Since I used the SIM card example to explain the effect of providing even one service, there is one more similarity in both scenarios. I'm always amazed by the way Jio entered and disrupted the industry. They launched with an unbelievable offer that one could not refuse—a free SIM card for a year. This led to many people queuing up outside Jio centres across the country, not bothering about the speed or coverage of the network. In fact, it gave birth to many first-time internet users. This free trick worked extremely well and helped them get tons of people within weeks, enough to compete against players who had decades of establishment. People knew it was going to be free only for a limited time, but they just wanted to enjoy the free ride for as long as they could. But as a business, what happens after the free year is critical. Here's the point: the exit cost for a SIM card is extremely high. You have to call one number, then message another number, deal with tons of spam calls from the company you want to quit, clear all dues, go to a store with all the documents, get a KYC done, etc. It's a cumbersome process, and once you switch, you can't switch again for three months. If the new network turns out to be worse, you're stuck. But Jio was smart. After the free period ended, they took advantage of the high exit cost and further priced their plans so low that it changed the dynamics of the industry. They forced the competition to lower their prices to stay relevant in the market, ultimately becoming the industry leader.

This mirrors the automotive industry, but there's a significant difference. Here, it often adds a negative value. When someone gets any work done after spending a lot on labour and parts, they are bound to return to the same garage if something goes wrong. The car owner expects the garage to fix the problem without charging additional labour. If they go to another workshop, they'll be charged just for getting it checked, let alone fixing the issue. This tendency leads to getting other work done in the same garage. People have a perception that the garage, having prior context about the car, is best suited to handle any further problems. However, in reality, mechanics don't always remember the minute details that can impact the car's performance. The primary driver for customer retention in this case stems from the desire to avoid paying for the garage's mistake if they switch to a different garage or service centre. For garages, it becomes critical to maintain a positive reputation because if a customer has a negative experience, they're likely to spread the word, potentially harming the garage's image among their acquaintances or in the community. This word-of-mouth impact can significantly affect a garage's business and customer acquisition. Context switching is crucial in the automotive field; better context switching leads to more personalised service for that specific car, ultimately saving the car owner from potentially higher costs in the long run, and dealerships have established this infrastructure that works well for common periodic replacements.

8/10 car owners I have met and worked with people who "feel" that they have been cheated more than once throughout their ownership of that specific vehicle. Now let's understand what leads to this particular feeling. The number one reason is a lack of understanding regarding the repairs. It has always been like you send a car for periodic service or a repair and get it back with a piece of paper that asks you to pay ₹15,000, and that amount is a big expense for most Indian households that own a car. While the mechanic or advisor will read out the bill for you and, in most cases, will do the work only after you approve the jobs, they always talk as if you know what a balance rod bush is and where and why it is used in the car, assuming a level of knowledge that many car owners do not possess and that clearly is not enough. Some dealerships choose to provide details on a job card to illustrate estimates. However, many still rely on traditional methods, simply jotting down information on a piece of paper. This communication gap between service providers and car owners can create a sense of ambiguity, fostering the perception of being taken advantage of during car maintenance or repairs. For instance, check out the way an estimate was given to us at a Maruti Suzuki authorised workshop lately.

Perodic mentence Service — 2290
Engine oil — ~~480~~ 4200
oil filtr — 100
D·Bolt — 80
All consuable checkup — 200
W/A — 200 — 515
W1B — 450
TR
Brake Service
calipr pin Gressing — 850
All Door lubricaten — 450
____
9774 with GST

Some car dealerships are trying to be more transparent by sending repair estimates through WhatsApp as PDFs. However, one challenge is that customers usually can't see what's happening to their cars while they're being worked on. As I mentioned earlier, the customer can only check the cosmetic jobs properly and only feel the difference in experience post-relevant repair. For example, a clutch can feel smooth after it's replaced, but dealerships often don't let customers near the working area, making people wonder what's really going on with their cars. Another view on this is that while this lack of visibility makes customers sceptical and unsure about whether the work being done is necessary or fair, even if they were allowed near the car during repairs, they might only be able to verify that the requested work is being done. The ability to find out if only necessary jobs are done is something no customer can point out. Car repairs are often based on addressing symptoms, and once the visible issue is resolved, customers may assume everything is fine. The intricate details of what's done inside the car might not be of much interest to the car owner as long as the apparent problem is fixed.

Technological tax

In Kalyan, within our operational area, you'll find "Wheel Life NX," a wheel alignment and balancing shop that stands out. It's got all the machines you'd expect, but what sets it apart is Vijay, the guy they call "rassi alignment wala" (rope alignment person). Unlike the other shops relying on machines, Vijay does it differently; he uses a rope to spot misalignments, and people trust his expertise. Vijay takes it up a notch by throwing in a complimentary check-up within a month of your wheel alignment and balancing service. To keep track, he slaps a small sticker on your driver's sun visor. That sticker does double duty, letting Vijay and you know the next date and kilometres for your next wheel alignment and balancing.

Vijay keeps things organised with bundles of these stickers on a standing table. He jots down your bill for the car on the same table. It's a breeze - quick data entry on the sticker takes just a fraction of the time. When your car rolls in next time, Vijay doesn't need a computer. He just leans into your car from the driver's window, checks the last sticker, and figures out if your car qualifies for that free check-up. Smooth and efficient, just the way he rolls.

Technological tax

In a recent experimental endeavour, we aimed to streamline and enhance the entire process at "Wheel Life NX" using technology. The idea was to optimise the workflow, utilise recorded user data for timely reminders about tire changes, alignment, and balancing, and explore cross-selling opportunities with local shops in the city to boost customer engagement. To execute this, we provided Vijay with stickers of similar size but with a tech twist: each sticker had a QR code and a unique number printed on it. Vijay simply stuck the QR code sticker in the car's designated spot and noted the unique number on the bill. Behind the scenes, the QR code connected to a progressive web app, delivering an app-like experience for users. The app featured a straightforward design, particularly emphasizing the rewards section. However, recognizing that not everyone is familiar with QR code scanning, we devised a solution. Alongside the QR code, we planned to include a small banner. Vijay, being the face of the shop, would assist customers in scanning the QR code. Upon successful scanning, a human (one of us) would instantly connect through a video, guiding and engaging with the customer. This personalised touch aimed to bridge the gap between technology and human interaction, ensuring a seamless and user-friendly experience.

Towards the day's end, our routine involved a visit to Vijay's shop to gather all the carbon copies of the bills he had generated. These bills contained crucial information such as car details, the unique sticker number for app customization, and most importantly, the customer's phone number. Armed with this data, we initiated a personalised outreach strategy, calling each customer to introduce the app and highlight the immediate benefits and rewards they could enjoy.

However, delving into Vijay's perspective sheds light on a nuanced challenge. Vijay, along with his assistant, remained deeply engrossed in their work throughout the day. Anything introducing short-term friction was unwelcome, despite the potential long-term gains. Even with the QR code, nothing could beat the speed of Vijay's traditional method – peeping through the window to assess the status of a car's wheel alignment and balancing. Yet, in a surprising turn, Vijay chose to adopt the QR code sticker alongside his traditional one, doubling the time spent. Why? He saw the potential in using the QR code for timely reminders, attracting customers for tire purchases, and more, while his traditional sticker continued to serve the purpose of quick visual assessments. This serves as a prime example of how technology, while offering long-term benefits, imposes a significant operational tax in the automotive industry, impacting both the diverse spectrum of car owners and the frontline and backend workforce of any workshop.

The history of auto tech startups in India is closely tied to a realisation about the technological gaps present in third-party garages. Autotech entrepreneurs recognized that many traditional garages were lagging behind in terms of technology, presenting an opportunity to bring this sector online. In various pitches, entrepreneurs often highlighted this technological disparity by drawing comparisons to other online services. A common theme was expressed with statements like, "Today you order food online, get a cab with a few taps on your phone, and even find a girlfriend online, but managing and maintaining your car is still a cumbersome process."

While I believe this comparison might capture the essence of the problem, I would highly argue about the lack of digitization in the automotive maintenance sector and that managing a car is inherently different from ordering food or hailing a cab, and a direct analogy may not be entirely accurate. Over the years, however, the growth and market share of autotech solutions that have gone digital speak for themselves. Entrepreneurs, including myself, have seized the opportunity to bridge the technological gap in the automotive industry, and the year-over-year growth of online platforms has been substantial. The COVID-19 pandemic further accelerated the shift towards a digital-first approach, as people had limited options but to adopt online solutions for their everyday needs. This period witnessed a surge in internet users who, for the first time, began unlocking their phones with the hope of accomplishing tasks without interacting with humans directly.

Yet, the narrative around using technology solely for the sake of bringing a task to the digital realm is a viewpoint I personally challenge. Many argue that viewing technology as merely an enabler for mass problem-solving skips a crucial step: solving the problem for a few individuals first. This perspective emphasises the importance of addressing the specific needs of a few before scaling up to serve the masses effectively.

The emergence of garage aggregators stems from a unanimous acknowledgment of the broken state of the autocare or after-sales market in India, particularly concerning third-party workshops. This sector is notorious for being highly unorganised, lacking transparency, and inconvenient, although it offers cost-effective solutions. The prevalence of these workshops has resulted in a substantial portion of the market being controlled by them.

Entrepreneurs entering this domain recognized these challenges and envisioned a transformation by bringing everything online. They believed that by addressing these issues, especially the unorganised nature of the market, people would flock to their platforms. However, they were keen on retaining the cost-effective aspect of third-party workshops while attempting to turn a profit. Given the competitive landscape in India, where discounts and coupons are integral to building a customer base, these startups initially positioned themselves as "discount companies." The goal was to not only provide a solution to the existing problems but also influence the behaviour of a significant number of individuals within the automotive vertical.

Despite the availability of discounts through these platforms, there remains a segment of the population that avoids dealerships to circumvent the 18% GST on labour, which is already a significant expense for them. This scepticism extends to applications as well, as some individuals assume similar cost implications and, as a result, prefer to stay away from them. Consequently, creating awareness about the benefits of these platforms becomes as crucial as promoting the discounts they offer.

Changing entrenched human behaviour, particularly when key players are entrenched and comfortable, is a challenging and resource-intensive endeavour that demands both time and substantial investment.

Recognizing the technological gaps in many garages, companies decided to create a digital bridge between these garages and car owners—an application. They partnered with nearby garages, selecting them more for their appearance than other factors. Important things customers usually care about in a garage? Well, those got put on the back burner—it'd take too much time to inspect each one.

Here's a little secret: in India, not many folks care about how a garage looks. Garage owners aren't eager to splurge on fancy interiors because, funny enough, if a garage looks too posh, people assume it's pricey and tend not to show up. Armed with funding, these companies went all out marketing this digital bridge to people and took a cut from those who decided on a garage through it. And here's another insider tip: **The commission model doesn't work in this industry.** Am I really suggesting that the entire foundation on which numerous companies emerged and secured funding doesn't work? Yes, unfortunately, it's the case in this context. Does it work in other parts of this industry? Yes, and I'll dive into that in a bit.

Have you ever booked a cab through an app and found yourself in a situation where, once inside, the driver asks about your destination and the fare displayed on the app? Suppose the app showed ₹1000 for your ride. The driver then offers to take you to the exact same location for ₹850, but with a condition: you need to cancel the ride on the application.

Most passengers, including myself, might be tempted by this offer because a straightforward 15% discount sounds appealing. In this scenario, the driver explains that they would have to pay a 25% commission to the app for bringing you, ultimately receiving only ₹750 in total earnings. On the other hand, with their offer, the driver gets to earn more, and you get to pay less, creating a clear win-win situation for both parties.

This practice reveals how drivers often try to bypass the app to maximise their earnings and provide passengers with a more attractive deal, resulting in a mutually beneficial outcome for both the passenger and the driver. In the bustling world of autocare apps, Rajesh's story unfolds as a quintessential example. A seasoned manager at a major marketing company, Rajesh stands out not only for his professional acumen but also for his keen embrace of the digital landscape. His position in the marketing realm equips him with a sophisticated, digital-first mindset, making him an ideal candidate to explore innovative solutions in the autocare domain.

At the heart of Rajesh's automotive tale is his trusty Hyundai i20, a 2011 model that has clocked a modest 58,000 km. However, the seemingly low mileage is a deliberate choice on Rajesh's part. For his daily commute to the office, he strategically opts for the train, finding it not only practical but also economically savvy. The car, a prized possession, truly comes to life on weekends, transforming into the vehicle of choice for family escapades. Despite his attachment to the car, Rajesh's pragmatic approach to vehicle usage translates into a conscious effort to minimise expenses. With the majority of kilometres accumulating during family outings, he recognizes the need for an autocare solution that aligns with his cost-sensitive mindset. In his search for a suitable app, Rajesh sets his sights on one that not only caters to his specific needs but also offers enticing discounts, making the entire ownership experience more economical.

The turning point in Rajesh's autocare journey comes when he stumbles upon the perfect app, a digital haven promising significant discounts on essential services. Intrigued and motivated by the prospect of optimising his car maintenance costs, Rajesh wastes no time and swiftly books a service appointment for the upcoming weekend. Choosing this time ensures that he can be present at home, ready to pay attention to the servicing process and intervene if necessary. As the day unfolds, two representatives from the autocare company arrive at Rajesh's parking lot, ready to take his Hyundai i20 to the garage. These two individuals, emblematic of the company's commitment to service, efficiently secure the vehicle and take it to the designated garage. Meanwhile, Rajesh is introduced to his virtual companion, a dedicated virtual assistant assigned by the company. This virtual entity excels in communication, providing Rajesh with real-time updates through the app, fostering transparency and assurance throughout the entire process.

Later in the afternoon, with a house chore on his agenda, Rajesh plans to visit the garage. In some instances, customers might harbour past grievances, especially if they've had a negative experience with the same garage. However, Rajesh harbours no such concerns. His proactive approach stems from a genuine curiosity about the ongoing maintenance of his car. Upon reaching the garage, Rajesh engages with the mechanic to gain insights into his car's current status. To his satisfaction, the mechanic not only provides a detailed overview of the identified issues but also presents a transparent approach by requesting Rajesh's approval through the app. This step initiates the estimation process, solidifying the collaborative nature of the autocare experience.

In the absence of any lingering concerns, Rajesh takes the opportunity to chat with the mechanic, establishing a personal connection. Their conversation transcends the transactional nature of the service, and Rajesh even secures the mechanic's phone number for future reference. As Rajesh makes his way back home, he does so with a sense of reassurance and confidence in the autocare process. The smooth communication, transparency, and positive interaction at the garage have not only met but exceeded his expectations, reinforcing the value of the autocare app in facilitating a seamless and customer-centric car maintenance journey. Following Rajesh's approval through the app, the virtual company representative promptly sends over the estimated cost. Rajesh gives the green light, and soon enough, his car is delivered right to his doorstep.

In some cases, a common scenario unfolds where the mechanic, while meeting the customer, reveals additional issues not reported during the pick-up. The mechanic might propose doing these extra jobs at a lower cost directly, subtly undermining the app's authority and sometimes criticising the company. Whether accurate or not, customers often tend to trust the mechanic more. Unlike a cab driver looking for extra income, the mechanic's motivation is not solely about making more money. Instead, it's a strategic move to build a connection with the customer, take charge of the relationship, and simplify the process outside of the complexities associated with internet companies. Fortunately, Rajesh's experience is free of such complications. After the smooth delivery, he takes his car for a spin and relishes the satisfaction of a hassle-free autocare journey.

As Rajesh's car gets older, just like people do, it starts having some unexpected problems. About a month after its regular service, Rajesh notices a strange issue. Every time he turns the car around, a weird "kharrrrrrrrrrrrrrrrrrrrrrrrrrr" sound comes from the front left side of his car, making him worry about the car's condition. Can you understand what that problem could be? Explaining such specific problems in writing, no matter how good you are at it, can be really hard. Realising this, Rajesh chooses an easier way. Instead of using the app to write about the problem, he simply calls the mechanic. When the mechanic picks up the call, Rajesh says, "Main Rajesh bol raha hu i20, application se aaya tha service ke liye yaad aaya?" (This is Rajesh speaking; I came through the app for service, do you remember?). Even if the mechanic doesn't remember Rajesh right away, he still says in a friendly way, "Haa sir, bolo kya hua?" (Yes, sir, tell me, what happened?). Rajesh then tells him, "Gaadi mein kuch aawaz aara hai left side se" (There's a noise coming from the left side of the car). The mechanic quickly responds, "Ok sir, gaadi leke aajao main dekh lunga kya hai" (Alright sir, bring the car, I'll take a look).

After this conversation, Rajesh decides to go to the garage over the weekend. This way, he can quickly deal with the new problem and follow his preference for being more hands-on with his car. Looking forward to a solution that will fix his car's issue, Rajesh anticipates his upcoming visit to the garage. In the course of this journey, the app, which initially played a crucial role in helping Rajesh discover a suitable garage, seemingly faded into the background. While the app provided structure and documentation through PDFs, the true essence of the autocare experience emerged during the direct interactions with the mechanic. The mechanic's ability to establish a rapport with Rajesh became a pivotal factor. This connection led to direct calls when needed, bypassing the intermediary of the app. In this scenario, the app served as the initial facilitator, connecting Rajesh with the garage, but the real bond formed between the customer and the mechanic.

Now, as the mechanic strives to provide excellent service, there's a significant likelihood that Rajesh will become a loyal customer of this specific garage. The allure of personalised attention and a satisfactory experience may overshadow any discounts or conveniences offered by the app. This situation prompts a noteworthy opinion: "The automotive industry cannot be fully digitised beyond a point." The nuances of customer relationships, personalised service, and the intrinsic human element in car care go beyond what a digital platform can entirely replicate. The blend of technology and the hands-on expertise of a skilled mechanic seems to create a more robust and lasting connection in the realm of car maintenance.

While these platforms were initially designed to serve as convenient online booking facilities with the promise of an improved in-garage experience, their practical implementation faces challenges. The core issue lies in the dependency on individual garage owners to adhere to the app's specified processes and rules. The claim of full quality control and operational enhancement at the partnered garages can be challenging to achieve without direct oversight and control over the entire process. Relying on garage owners to follow the prescribed procedures introduces a level of uncertainty, as they operate independently and may not consistently align with the app's standards.

The remote supervision model, while offering convenience, can indeed create a gap between what is portrayed and the ground reality. Garage owners may showcase what the app wants to see, potentially deviating from actual practices. This dependence on garage owners may compromise the app's ability to ensure a standardised and quality-controlled experience across all service providers.

Garage folks can be pretty egoistic, and no such person would like sticking to rules. Even if you manage to convince a few, getting through to one garage, let alone 10 or 50, is a real uphill task and eats up a lot of time. Their resistance to following rules comes from their pride. They see apps as nothing more than tools to "fill in the blanks." To them, apps are just a way to fill up any empty space in the garage, not the main thing for getting new customers. This makes you wonder: do garage owners see apps as real partners in getting new customers, or just as handy tools to fill up empty spots? Now, some might say that struggling garages would welcome any extra customer. But here's the thing: in reality, apps are not too keen on tying up with garages that are not doing so well. It's like they're picky about who they partner with. This whole situation raises a big question in the autocare world. How can the industry find a middle ground between the pride of garage owners and the need for clear rules to make sure customers have a good and reliable experience? It's a tricky balance to strike.

Garages operating within the app ecosystem often face limitations and lack independence. The app typically conceals the garage branding, preventing them from establishing a distinct identity. Additionally, various restrictions are imposed on their workflow by the app, shaping the way they operate within the platform. This lack of independence can be a point of disagreement for garages, as it restricts their ability to build a unique brand presence and operate autonomously. The app's control over branding and workflow may impact how garages are perceived by customers and limit their flexibility in providing services.

When it comes to Zomato and restaurants, there's a common expectation that the app will be a major way to get new customers. So, when a new restaurant opens up, they usually reach out to Zomato themselves to get listed on the app. It's a kind of natural process for restaurants on Zomato. Now, things work a bit differently with garages. Unlike restaurants, tying up with autocare apps isn't a continuous thing for garages. The app needs to actively search for and partner with garages, which requires ongoing effort and consistent work. It's not like garages will automatically come to the app; the app has to actively discover and connect with them.

On the app, the primary goal is to encourage users to book their regular car service. Following that, the app provides additional beneficial services such as various cleaning options, tire and battery services, AC maintenance, and more. What's interesting is that all these services are super specific and can be easily understood by any car owner.

The specific nature of certain automotive tasks, like booking regular services, makes them well-suited for digitization. However, when it comes to issues like the noise Rajesh experienced from the left side, these problems are symptom-based and require more hands-on work for effective communication, diagnosis, and quality checks. Managing such complexities through an application appears inefficient and involves a significant learning curve. Surprisingly, the automotive industry thrives on human-to-human interactions and offline engagement, which resonates with many people. They appreciate the lack of an extra learning curve in this domain. Consequently, while these apps may excel at handling specific tasks, relying on them for every aspect of car care seems like a distant goal. The intricate nature of automotive issues demands a more personalised and hands-on approach that current digital platforms may not entirely fulfil. The adoption of autocare apps remains remarkably low, with a minimal number of people utilising these apps for car-related services. Several factors, including the reasons mentioned earlier, contribute to car owners not prioritising or caring about these apps. The infrequency of periodic services, usually occurring once a year for most users, adds an extra layer of friction. Additionally, the utilisation of value-added services beyond periodic maintenance is limited, as only a small percentage of individuals spend money outside of the annual service.

Apps that achieve more than two uses per month fall into the bracket where they can try and create a habit. Attempting to create a habit in users becomes more difficult with lower frequency, as there's a higher likelihood that users may forget about the app. The limited time available to educate users about offerings, coupled with the challenge of gaining insights from infrequent engagements, makes monetization and creating a viable, scalable business exceptionally challenging. Achieving good retention in this context becomes extremely crucial, yet even more difficult due to the low level of user engagement, and the reality is that many people simply do not care about autocare apps. Most apps offer user flows that can be easily replicated on widely used platforms like WhatsApp, which serves as an effective medium to initiate digitization while minimising the learning curve and aligning with a truly customer-centric mindset. Products with infrequent use patterns are essentially utility products, addressing pain points that occur episodically for customers. In many cases, the product or service is already successfully offered and consumed in the non-digital, offline world through physical businesses.

Contrary to the conventional emphasis on retention as a crucial metric, Viveck Kumar, the author of the ICED theory, suggests that for infrequent products, the more pivotal metric is "penetration." In this context, retention might not apply in the traditional sense. According to Kumar, the measure of product-market fit is best gauged by increasing the number of transactions, indicating market penetration. A good example here is Airbnb. He highlights that the main focus is on the number of nights booked, but there's also an interest in bringing users back to the platform for future bookings. This perspective shifts the emphasis from retaining users through frequent engagement to penetrating the market and increasing the overall number of transactions, aligning with the unique dynamics of infrequent product usage.

While I agree with the emphasis on penetration for infrequent products, it's crucial to recognize that retention plays a pivotal role in scenarios where users might return, even if infrequently. Using the example of Airbnb, a person may book accommodation again in the future, and their decision is often influenced by their initial experience with multiple factors on the platform. A positive first experience can significantly impact the likelihood of a user returning, even for infrequent transactions.

In the case of edtech apps, the dynamics differ. For example, someone preparing for UPSC and subscribing to a course on an edtech app is unlikely to purchase the same course again. In such cases, the app knows from day one that the user's engagement is finite and that retention metrics might not be as relevant. The nature of the product or service and the user's intent can shape the importance of retention in different contexts.

Let me talk in the context of infrequent products, particularly in the automotive industry, where tracking retention can indeed be challenging. However, the unique advantage in this scenario is the ability to precisely identify when a car owner will likely require the core offering, such as a periodic service. This enables personalised and highly relevant outreach. To approach the retention metric, considering the determinability of the annual periodic service is a strategic move. One way to analyse this from a macro standpoint is to track the service-to-year ratio. Instead of a strict 12-month cycle, opting for a 15-month time frame accommodates potential delays in service appointments. This ratio can provide insights into how many cars undergo the service within a 15-month period, offering a comprehensive view of retention dynamics within the context of the automotive industry. This approach aligns with the inherent infrequency of the product while capturing the patterns and behaviours relevant to the service cycle. This indeed poses a unique challenge to the concept of minimum viable product (MVP). While traditional MVPs are often seen as short stints to validate hypotheses, the nature of the automotive industry requires a more extended period, typically at least 15 months, to gather meaningful user insights, especially considering the service-to-year ratio.

From my perspective, achieving true product-market fit (PMF) in the automotive industry is yet to be accomplished by any app. This challenge persists because, in my view, sustainable strategies have not been adequately explored. Evaluating the service-to-year ratio of any app often reveals a notable deficiency. It's rare to find even a 5-month MVP duration, let alone 15 months, and the absence of a budget for research and development within this timeframe emerges as a significant factor. Among the millions of downloads celebrated by these apps and the impressive vendor tie-up statistics they showcase, the reality is that the conversion of users into sticky, regular users is considerably lower. The apps aspire for car owners to download and commence usage well before their service is due. This approach serves two purposes: first, it enables the apps to achieve high engagement levels, and second, it allows them to build trust with users until their service is due, increasing the likelihood of them choosing the app when the time comes.

So, in the effort to achieve that, autocare apps strategically introduce a variety of features, and this acts similar to the role of milk in local stores, which does not bring much profit but great footfall. Similarly, these apps use a mix of features to keep users engaged. These features include Fastag services, tracking insurance, easy management of PUC and challans, simple EMI calculators, access to fuel costs across the country, and the ability to book a test drive for a new car.

Moreover, these apps spend a good chunk of their budget on effective marketing, ensuring a consistent and noticeable presence in the market. This strategic approach not only aims to build trust but also to establish a recognizable identity in users' minds well before their service is due, creating a lasting impact.

By taking this approach, autocare apps aim to enhance the user experience by offering a comprehensive set of services beyond the basic periodic service. The goal is to become essential companions for car owners, providing a smooth and reliable journey in their automotive care endeavours. In addition to earning commissions from garages, autocare apps find another lucrative revenue stream in the spare parts market. Many of these apps aim to monopolise the supply of spare parts for the cars serviced through their platform. To achieve this, they establish partnerships with factories to brand common items such as oil, tools, oil filters, and more. Through this strategy, they can command higher profit margins, which vary depending on the brand and the product. Given the relatively low daily intake on their platform, these apps also explore selling spare parts to all garages, regardless of their tie-up status with the app. This dual approach allows them to maximise their revenue potential in the spare parts segment of the autocare industry.

Technological tax

In the current scenario, local garages typically have their preferred vendors who promptly provide information on the price and availability of specific parts over a quick call, and upon confirmation, the garage can swiftly visit the local shop to acquire the required parts. On the other hand, some autocare apps maintain a spare part inventory, a challenging task, especially concerning cataloguing. These inventories are usually set up in locations accessible from multiple areas with affordable real estate. However, they may not be as accessible to garages as their local counterparts. The process of obtaining parts from the app's inventory introduces more friction compared to the seamless experience offered by local spare part vendors. Moreover, original equipment manufacturer (OEM) parts generally yield minimal margins, typically below 5%, for garages. When autocare apps aim for rapid growth, they often offer substantial discounts, creating the impression among garages that the parts being sold may not be genuine.

Besides spare parts, these apps generate revenue through advertisements. They generate new car leads, forwarding them to partner dealerships for a commission. Additionally, brands promoting products like batteries and accessories are featured in banners, occasionally accompanied by exclusive offers on the app to stimulate sales.

Nevertheless, there are numerous untapped avenues for revenue generation, especially in the B2B segment. Autocare apps could explore partnerships with cab-hailing companies and local tours and travel operators, providing their drivers with competitive pricing and nationwide support. Caradvise, operating in the US, is a prime example of a company successfully venturing into this space. Another lucrative opportunity that is not common lies in the realm of recycling. Garages accumulate a considerable number of parts earmarked for scrapping, presenting an opportunity for individuals or businesses to capitalise on this resource and generate income.

Presently, autocare apps are grappling with the challenge of establishing lasting relationships with car owners and minimising switching costs, as evidenced by Rajesh's experience. The failures and abrupt closures of some apps, leaving debts with numerous vendors, have cast a shadow over the perception of new startups attempting to address these issues. There is a prevailing scepticism and suspicion among vendors and car owners towards app-based car maintenance services. Many view them as potential scams and harbour the belief that these apps merely adopt a common model of partnering with third-party garages. This negative perception poses a considerable obstacle for emerging startups in the industry.

If the autocare industry is characterised by being unorganised, inconvenient, and time-consuming, and if having car owners present during the service addresses the issues of inconvenience and turns the process into a satisfactory one, it raises a valid question. Considering that most cars typically require servicing only once a year, taking out 3 hours over a weekend for this purpose seems like a reasonable and manageable commitment. This approach not only ensures that car owners actively engage in the care of their vehicles but also contributes to a more organised and satisfactory autocare experience for themselves. Users opt for these car apps instead of the traditional garage approach mainly for two reasons. Firstly, they seek to sidestep the hassle of searching for a reliable garage, and the app assures them time savings by managing the entire process. This convenience becomes especially beneficial for those with packed schedules, and the app's promise to handle everything aligns well with their busy lifestyles.

Secondly, users are on the lookout for enticing deals, particularly for specific car-related tasks. The app becomes a platform not just for convenience but also for accessing attractive offers, adding an extra layer of value for its users. This desire for both convenience and savings reflects a practical mindset among individuals who prefer efficient digital solutions for their daily tasks. Therefore, for those navigating a hectic schedule, being tech-savvy, and appreciating streamlined processes, engaging with an app representative, known for effective communication, becomes a logical and time-efficient choice. The app not only simplifies the autocare process but also resonates with users seeking a balance between convenience and cost-effectiveness in managing their car-related needs.

Now that sounds like a smaller market size than the original thought of digitising the entire automotive ecosystem. So what really is the market size of these apps in India? As mentioned earlier, every car owner, especially after the warranty of the car expires, falls into one of these three categories: dealership preference, a specific third-party preference, or no preference. The real market size of the apps is just a small chunk of car owners who do not have any preference for a garage; they think in a direction where, rather than relying on any random garage, they anticipate a more organised and enhanced experience through the app. To be more precise, this group is primarily composed of individuals who are time-constrained, relying on various apps for their daily chores. Their decision to use autocare apps stems from the expectation of a more efficient and organised solution for their car maintenance needs. This segment values the convenience and tech-savvy approach offered by autocare apps, making them a distinct and targeted audience within the automotive landscape. Indeed, another significant segment comprises individuals who prefer going to dealerships simply to avoid the hassle of selecting and dealing with any random garage. This group, too, forms an appropriate persona for autocare apps, and I believe these individuals are prime candidates who would find great satisfaction in using the app. Autocare apps offer them the convenience of a streamlined process without the need to navigate through the challenges of selecting a garage. This particular group values the ease and efficiency that autocare apps bring to their car maintenance experience, making them a pivotal audience for the success and adoption of these applications.

Addressing the market dynamics, a notable challenge emerges from the strategy adopted by many autocare apps during their market entry. Several have attempted to establish themselves by criticising third-party workshops, labelling them as users of duplicate parts, and denouncing dealerships as overpriced. In my perspective, this approach might be counterproductive. Both third-party workshops and dealerships have long-standing control over the autocare market, and attempting to gain traction by defaming them appears to be an unwise move.

An interesting point to consider is that the garages these apps tie up with often fall into the same category of third-party workshops. This raises a valid question: Is this approach somewhat hypocritical? The answer to that may vary, and it's a nuanced consideration. Ultimately, the success of autocare apps may depend on a more balanced and constructive approach that respects the existing players in the market while highlighting the unique value propositions these apps bring to the table. Here is a screenshot from an estimate generated by GoMechanic for me.

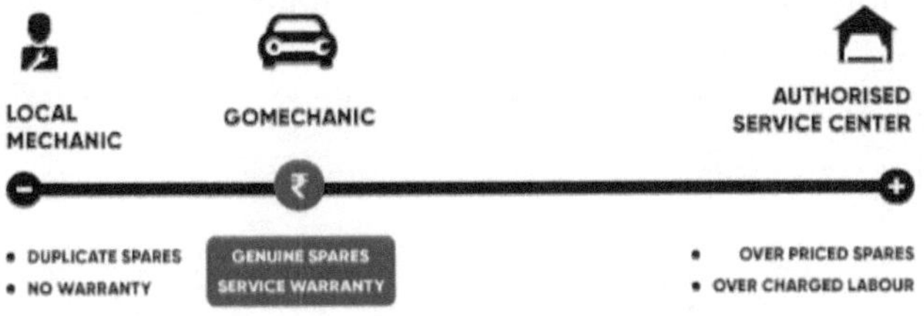

They probably use this on the last page of every estimate and invoice they generate.

Mistakes are an inherent part of any garage operation worldwide, and they are virtually unavoidable due to numerous factors, some of which are beyond the technician's control, while others depend on the technician's skills. For instance, during a suspension overhaul, a technician might unintentionally leave a nut bolt loose, leading to a worsening driving experience during the trial. This kind of error can instantly upset the customer. Another scenario could involve an old battery dying while the car is in the garage, leaving the customer with no choice but to incur additional costs to replace the battery. These unpredictable situations emphasise the complexity of automotive maintenance and the challenges faced by both technicians and customers alike.

An intriguing observation emerges in this context. When garages work directly with consumers and mistakes occur, they are generally willing to rectify the issue promptly. In such cases, they may even reopen the suspension or perform additional repairs as needed. This willingness stems from the fact that garages not only generate revenue from selling spare parts but are also responsible for the parts used in the repair, making them liable for ensuring customer satisfaction.

On the contrary, when working with an app aggregator, garages encounter a dual challenge. Not only do they lose revenue from the sale of spare parts, but they also have to pay a commission to the app for facilitating the service. This dynamic creates a nuanced situation where the financial considerations for garages become more complex, influencing their response to addressing mistakes and customer concerns. In situations where support work is necessitated by the customer, such as a sudden change in approval for a job or late communication, the responsibility for the additional work typically falls on the customer. The garage may charge the customer for the extra labour and time incurred due to the altered instructions.

On the other hand, if the need for rework arises from a faulty part supplied by the app during the post-work inspection, the responsibility often lies with the app. In such cases, the app is expected to cover the costs associated with rectifying the issue, including any labour charges and replacement parts. It is extremely important to ensure quality control and reliable part sourcing on the part of the app to minimise such situations and maintain a positive relationship with both garages and customers.

I just highlighted a challenging scenario for the app when it comes to negotiating rework costs with the garage. Indeed, garages may be reluctant to undertake additional work without expecting extra compensation, and rightfully so, considering the time and effort involved. In such situations, ensuring a fair resolution without burdening the customer becomes crucial. Unfortunately, ground reality often sees the garage finding ways to recover these additional costs from the customer, whether through subtle increases in charges or other means.

Navigating this delicate negotiation between the app and the garage while prioritising a positive customer experience requires a delicate balance and effective communication channels, and it becomes difficult to establish clear terms and conditions in agreements between apps and garages to manage such situations transparently and equitably, which benefits both! Hence, if the customer, a few days after the repair, encounters an issue and decides to approach the garage directly, they may do so willingly for minor problems. However, for more significant issues, they might prefer to go through the app. This experience can be highly frustrating for a car owner. They find themselves in a situation where they need to explain the problem over a phone call to someone who might not have firsthand knowledge of the specific circumstances. Determining whether it's the garage's fault, an issue with a part, or potentially the customer's fault adds another layer of complexity to the situation. This process can be cumbersome and challenging for the car owner, as well as for those trying to assess and resolve the problem remotely.

In the scenario of the suspension overhaul, where the initial inspection identified only the balance rod bushes for replacement, a potential challenge arises when, just a week later, the lower arm requires changing. While it's conceivable that external factors, such as the customer encountering a substantial pothole, could be the cause, there's a difficulty in directly attributing blame. The crucial issue here lies in the need for seamless context switching. Understanding real-time developments on the ground becomes pivotal to accurately assessing the situation. Achieving a smooth transition in comprehending these dynamic scenarios is essential for fair evaluations and effective problem resolution. Another significant challenge surfaces when customers, despite the garage performing the work, tend to attribute any subsequent issues to the app itself. This tendency creates dissatisfaction, as customers may hold the app responsible for problems even when external factors are at play. In such cases, customers may refrain from returning unless they experience a swift and satisfactory resolution. Navigating this challenge involves not only effective communication and transparent explanations but also ensuring prompt resolutions. Maintaining customer trust within the autocare app ecosystem hinges on addressing these attribution challenges and providing timely solutions for customer satisfaction.

Even if the matter escalates to a legal context, where the app can point to the disclaimer signed by the car owner absolving the app of responsibility for the garage's work, courts might rule in favour of the car owner. This tendency might stem from the notion that if someone receives payment, they are likely to be held accountable. You see, there will always be some customers who will just make your life difficult at every step, and while some garages may have the liberty to refuse service to such customers, for a mass adoption-focused application, this option is simply out of the picture. As a result, the app must invest significant time and resources to establish trust with every car owner. It's crucial to ensure that each user understands the roles and responsibilities, clarifying whose accountability they can hold if any issues arise. This proactive approach becomes essential for building a robust relationship between the app, the garages, and the car owners, fostering trust, and minimising any potential legal disputes.

The autocare industry, particularly autocare apps, seems to have overlooked the significant role of research and development (R&D) in their evolution. While big hardware companies allocate substantial budgets for R&D, autocare apps may have taken a considerable gamble by focusing more on digitization than on substantial improvements to the traditional and often chaotic processes. The emphasis on digitization, while crucial, may have overshadowed the importance of establishing a well-controlled network on the ground to facilitate smooth operations.

Many folks seem to overlook the importance of a well-organised operational network, leading to a less-than-smooth experience in different parts of the car world. It looks like disorder in operations is quite common, and being able to carry out tasks quickly and effectively is seen as really important. Making sure things run smoothly on the ground could give companies in the autocare business a big edge, like a protective barrier, setting them apart from the competition.

Nimbu mirchi

As we delve deeper into this discussion, it should become increasingly evident that the significance of a car extends far beyond its basic function as a mode of transportation in Indian culture. This cultural significance is apparent right from the moment of purchase. The new car is often welcomed with a traditional religious ceremony known as a pooja, and a string bearing a lemon (nimbu) and chilli (mirchi) is tied to the car. This ritual, deeply rooted in cultural belief, is performed with the firm belief that it will ward off any malevolent forces or the 'evil eye' that might threaten the well-being of the vehicle or its occupants, setting the tone for the relationship between the car and its owner.

The diversity among car owners in India is quite remarkable. There's a wide spectrum of attitudes and behaviours when it comes to car management. Some people meticulously plan a budget for their car repairs, similar to how it would sound if one planned a budget for a medical procedure before they even visited a doctor. This practice, while it may appear weird to some, is quite common in India.

Furthermore, it's not unusual to encounter individuals who, despite years of driving experience, may not be familiar with basic vehicle operations. For instance, they might not know how to de-engage the steering lock and may need to call upon a mechanic for assistance with such straightforward tasks. This tendency to seek reassurance and confirmation from others for even the simplest things is quite prevalent.

An interesting cultural practice among some Indian car owners is to keep the plastic covers on their car seats for as long as they own the vehicle. It might seem unusual to some, but this habit is surprisingly common in India. The reason behind it for some people is to create the impression that the car is brand new, regardless of its actual age or usage.

Understanding the behaviours and attitudes of Indian car consumers is no small feat, considering the wide array of practices and approaches to car management. In an attempt to simplify this complex landscape, I introduced the 2x2 framework in a previous discussion. This framework categorises people based on their level of discipline towards managing their car and their choice of workshop. The framework, which I have named the "Magical square of Mekit," serves as an effective tool for explaining the various types of consumers and aids in understanding their suitability for different types of automotive apps. It can also be applied to understand workshop preferences in a broader context.

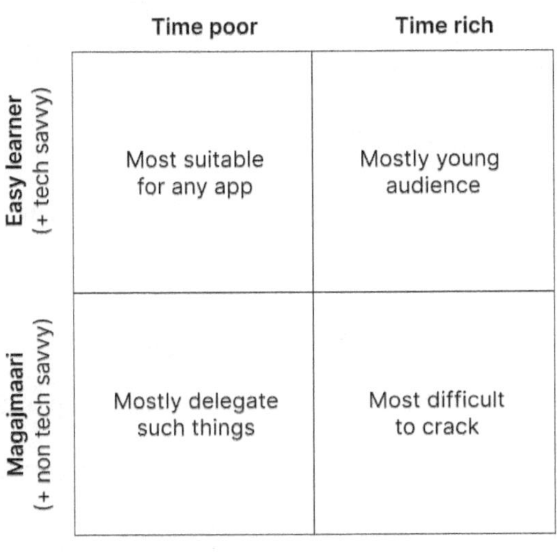

Humans are lazy in the sense that they don't want to invest time and energy to unwrap and understand what something is. No patience to read directions. No time to deviate. Life has such a steep learning curve as it is, with seldom enough time for work, play, learning, and love. And so, when something entirely new requires too much effort, they just let it pass. Their default is to avoid things that take effort until we're convinced of the benefits. This reference by Scott Belsky very well explains what I mean by magajmaari in this context.

a. Time poor and easy learner.

This is the ideal demographic for any app or workshop consisting of individuals who lead busy, active lives. These are people who are typically engaged in full-time employment, run their own businesses, or operate as professionals in their respective fields. One common denominator among this group is that they are often the primary owners of the car, and as such, they are the ones responsible for the majority of the expenses associated with the vehicle.

Some notable characteristics of this demographic include the frequent use of credit cards and a subscription to at least two or three top-tier OTT platforms. They generally prefer communication via chat, owing to their fast-paced lifestyle and the convenience it offers. Time is a precious commodity for them, and they place a high value on services that can help them save time. They are typically willing to pay for these time-saving services and appreciate their value.

In addition, these individuals possess a basic understanding of car maintenance and are ready to invest the necessary resources in its upkeep. They have the financial capacity to do so and are willing to spend as required without constantly seeking significant discounts. This discerning, sophisticated demographic is the dream audience of every app and workshop, as they recognize the value of the services offered and are willing to invest in them. Other traits include being chat friendly, speaking decent english, might have a LinkedIn account, a Spotify or Apple music subscription, mostly born after 1982, they are the ones who might ask for a GST bill, live in tier 1 societies, might as well own more than one car, less likely to pick calls from an unknown number and don't mind pre-paying for ecommerce orders. These people are relatively easier to build trust with and make financial decisions themselves making them a dream audience for most b2c apps out there.

b. Time rich and easy learner.

These are individuals who are technologically smart, able to quickly understand and utilise new concepts and tools. These individuals often have an abundance of time to dedicate to learning and exploration. This group predominantly falls within the younger demographic, generally under the age of 26. A smaller portion of this group also comprises older individuals retired or on sabbatical, usually over the age of 55, who often have children living away from home. This necessitates their need to become more tech-savvy in order to maintain communication and connection with their distant loved ones.

However, when it comes to the younger demographic, it is important to note that while they may be the primary users of the technology, they are often not the decision-makers, especially in financial matters such as car purchases. They tend to act as intermediaries between the technology and the actual owner of the car, who is often their parent.

Despite not being the final decision-makers, these young individuals play a crucial role in introducing new applications and technological advances to their parents. Nevertheless, while their role as influencers is valuable, it is not recommended to focus marketing efforts on them. Instead, it would be more beneficial to utilise them as a conduit to reach the actual decision-maker or owner. This allows for a more effective use of resources, targeting the individuals who have the financial authority to approve purchases and investments. Other traits of people in the category include being an active user on Snapchat and Instagram, having a dedicated slot daily to spend time with friends, ordering ecommerce goods with COD option so that someone else in the house can pay for the product upon delivery.

c. Time poor and magajmaari.

These individuals, despite their lack of time, are not particularly tech-savvy. For these individuals, dealing with any technological element they don't understand can quickly become an overwhelming mental strain, a situation they refer to as 'magajmaari'. To avoid the mental effort and the potential confusion, they often delegate these tasks to others (mainly the time rich and easy learner category), only stepping in when it comes time to pay the bills. This approach to avoiding the hassle also extends to their handling of car maintenance, where they prefer to hand over their vehicles to a dealership just to avoid any learning curve, and they do it usually during the weekends when they have more free time to be present and communicate their needs. Their preference stems from the convenience of being at home during these times, making it easier for them to supervise the process. They hardly read any reports or estimates, instead expecting all necessary information to be relayed to them via a phone call. They trust the professionals to do their job and keep them informed. This is a common trend I have observed among a significant number of low- and medium-level government officials. Moreover, I've also noticed this pattern among many individuals working in the private sector, especially those who have been employed by the same multinational corporation for over a decade. This is particularly prevalent among those residing in Tier 3 cities and beyond, where perhaps the pace of technological advancement might not be as rapid or as readily embraced as in the more urban areas. Some traits that you might find across these people are being active on Facebook more than Instagram, frequently listening to radio while driving their car, taking financial decisions after consulting with other people, preferring to generally take safe bets in multiple aspects of life, might pick calls from unknown numbers and generally ask for a bill wherever relevant.

d. Time rich and magajmaari.

These individuals are blessed with an abundance of time yet lack the necessary technological expertise, and consequently, do not expend effort in learning new skills or embracing modern technology. This group represents the most challenging demographic for any application to successfully engage and satisfy. Predominantly, these individuals are the ones who choose to stay with their vehicle at all times during a service or repair job, precisely due to their limited understanding of automotive mechanics and to make sure they are able to save money. Their lack of knowledge often results in unrealistic expectations and misattributions of newly arisen issues to prior repair work. For instance, they may blame an auto repair shop for their air conditioning not functioning adequately the following day, even though the shop had only performed a clutch assembly replacement. In addition to being technically challenged, these individuals tend to be extremely cost-conscious. They frequently bring their own parts to a repair job in an attempt to save money, place a higher value on cashback offers over convenience, and are always on the hunt for discounts. Their frugality occasionally borders on the extreme, and they are often reluctant to expend funds on convenience. Workshops and service centres themselves struggle to cater to the demands of these particular customers. These customers are akin to those who consistently order the same dish from the same restaurant yet constantly complain about the previous experience. Other traits in people of this category might include not respecting productivity, using telegram to download latest movies and web series against an OTT subscription, typically not studying after undergrad and are very difficult to monetise and gain trust. If any application can successfully navigate this challenging landscape, engage this difficult demographic, and also generate profit, the task of managing the aforementioned three groups would be significantly eased. This would represent a milestone achievement in the industry. There's also this super cool breakdown of Indian consumers in the Indus Valley Report. Some are even compared to whole countries! It's a mega-useful guide to understanding the whole Indian startup scene, and it's created by the genius minds at Blume Ventures. No matter what industry you're in, it's a must-read.

There are two key elements that are universally applicable to all four types of consumers we've identified, and any app seeking success in this space should invest significant effort into achieving both. The first element is trust-building. In today's climate, building trust is absolutely vital, especially given the high-stakes nature of automotive issues, which often carry significant emotional and financial weight. The landscape has been further complicated by previous startups, which have inadvertently eroded trust in the industry. Given that any failure in car repair can potentially risk lives, it's not an exaggeration to say that maintaining a relentless focus on quality and standardisation isn't just an option; it's a necessity. Consider the strategy employed by apps like CRED, which invest heavily in featuring credible, well-known personalities in their advertisements. It's clear communication to their potential users that transactions conducted on their platform are safe and can be trusted. Similarly, think about why a soap might be named after the river Ganga. It's a smart move that instantly associates the product with purity, despite the chemical composition being identical to any other soap in the market. In the context of the automotive industry, building trust requires a deep commitment to ethical practices that benefit all parties involved, from the car owner to the garage owner. One of the most effective ways to foster trust with a new user is through a referral. However, cultivating a scalable culture of personal referrals that yields high conversion rates can be difficult to achieve. Often, if a person is enthusiastically sharing information about a product, it's assumed they have some kind of incentive to do so. Similarly, people tend to approach workshops with a degree of scepticism.

But imagine if you could create an environment where garage owners are also referring your app to their customers. That would be the proverbial cherry on top and could potentially unlock the most powerful organic acquisition channel for your app. When something goes wrong with a car, the owner usually needs either a burnol (a reference to imply that the car owner needs to get out of that situation urgently with whatever help) if it is a very urgent problem or sinthol (from a soap name just because it rhymes well with burnol) if he just needs some guidance or clarity on how serious the issue is and what should be done at that very moment plus an approximate prediction of cost and the problem, mainly for non-breakdown or urgent problems. If any app can be a part of this scenario and solve it well for any consumer, they will very likely gain the car owner's trust. When a car has an issue, the owner often needs immediate assistance (referred to as 'burnol') for urgent problems or guidance and clarity (referred to as 'synthol') for less critical issues. This guidance includes understanding the seriousness of the issue, what should be done immediately, an approximate cost estimate, and an explanation of the problem. If an app can insert itself into this scenario and provide a satisfactory resolution, it stands a great chance of gaining the car owner's trust.

The second crucial factor out of the two major considerations is "cost efficiency." Regardless of any varying opinions, the predominant reason why someone opts to maintain their car at a third-party garage is primarily due to cost considerations, with customization standing as a secondary reason.

When a car owner decides to seek out a third-party workshop for their vehicle's maintenance, they are often motivated by the significantly lower rates compared to those offered by the dealership. They also look for creative, cost-effective solutions, or 'jugaad', as it's often termed, wherever possible instead of resorting to direct replacement of the part, which can be an expensive affair. In addition to this, the car owner can also overcome the additional 18% GST on the labour amount by choosing to go with a third-party workshop. The convenience of the workshop's closer proximity to their place of residence or work is an added advantage that cannot be disregarded. For the more refined or sophisticated customers, they operate with a cost-saving mindset. They think along the lines of, "If I can save money by opting for service A instead of service B for the same job, then why not?" On the other hand, the other three categories of customers are actively scouting for the most affordable pricing in the market. This is the principal reason why you will find low cost as the primary proposition in most car maintenance apps and even at dealerships. They first draw in the customer with attractive discounts so that the customer steps into the workshop. Once the customer is in, they then make up for the discount by charging extra for additional services or items. This strategy has been found to be quite effective in the car maintenance industry.

In every development of an application or workshop, we can take significant learning from the security guards or watchmen in societies who have indisputably dominated the exterior car washing market. These individuals rule this sector with such proficiency that it becomes nearly impossible for any washing centre or app to compete with them.

Their business model is astonishingly cost-efficient. They charge a modest monthly fee ranging from ₹500 to ₹800, regardless of the type of car. In return, you are guaranteed a shining car every morning, ready for your commute to the office. Trust is not an issue; in fact, it is part of their job to know each resident personally, and most often, they also take care of small chores upon request, so they already have a great rapport. Moreover, their operational costs are almost negligible. The essential tools of their trade—a bucket, water, and a cloth—are often arranged for free, eliminating the need for any significant capital expenditure. Despite the simplicity of their tools and methods, they consistently deliver impeccable results, satisfying the customer every morning, precisely on time. They cater to all four types of consumers, and most impressively, they manage to earn a salary equivalent to their monthly wages simply by dedicating 2-3 hours to washing cars daily. To provide a comparison, a single foam wash at a car washing centre for a hatchback starts at ₹300, and the price varies according to the size of the car and the infrastructure of the workshop. Take a look at the watchman in my building who is ruling his side hustle domain with simplicity and efficiency.

Clicked on 31 Jan 2024 at 8:33 am from my balcony.

People choose a garage with what I like to call the "panipuri mindset" (or golgappa, puchka, patashe, whichever term you prefer). It's like spotting the most crowded panipuri stall, assuming it must be tasty. Similarly, folks look for the most cost-efficient garage. The appearance of a garage plays a role, and hearing about it from someone you know or seeing its branding sticker on a car multiple times can seal the deal.

Think of it like the parking direction phenomenon. If you enter a parking zone and notice most cars are parked with their rear end to the wall, you might get influenced and park in the same way, even if there's no real reason for it. It's all about observing and following the crowd.

After selecting a garage, customers often get deeply involved in the initial interaction. This helps them evaluate the garage's suitability, both immediately and later after driving the car post-service. An interesting observation is that customers tend to have a better experience when their point of contact at the workshop shares their native place or is from the same region. While this doesn't practically impact the service, it significantly influences the customer's comfort level because they can communicate more easily in their regional language.

This idea of familiarity-enhancing customer experience is seen in other areas too. Take WhatsApp, for instance, which allows users to customise their chat wallpaper. While it doesn't have a concrete practical reason, it gives users a sense of personalization and ownership, fostering a positive connection with the platform—similar to the regional connection in a workshop.

Another intriguing insight into customer-garage dynamics is how assertive or aggressive customers are treated. Surprisingly, if a customer expresses anger or uses abrasive language, especially in a dealership, they often get prioritised over others as the dealership wants them to quickly leave and not let them spoil the environment. This suggests that maintaining a polite demeanour doesn't always guarantee the best service, which is somewhat disheartening.

There are also customers who resort to dishonest means for discounts or compensation. These individuals fabricate stories or exaggerate issues, posing a persistent challenge for the entire industry. Dealing with such deceitful tactics is tough. It's an unfortunate truth, but these individuals exist and create a constant hurdle for honest service providers.

The customer lounge in dealerships, which I think is no less than a kitty party, is an exceptional and unique place to gain a wealth of insights about consumers, particularly in high-volume dealerships like Maruti Suzuki, Tata, and Hyundai. These places offer a direct channel to listen to the customers' voices, their complaints, and their grievances. Issues raised frequently include customers feeling misled by dealerships, expressing their concerns about products not being suitable or adaptable to Indian roads, high costs, and more. Such places serve as a real-time feedback mechanism for companies to understand the ground reality and the actual experience of their consumers. I recently came across a profound quote on Twitter that read, "cheap labor is more expensive than expensive labor," which I believe is absolutely true.

In my day-to-day life, I've observed a lot of cars that have the Apple logo sticker displayed prominently on the rear windshield. This interesting phenomenon piqued my curiosity, and I found myself wanting to uncover the rationale behind this trend. The answer finally came to me during a casual conversation with a worker at one of our car washing partners.

He noticed the iPhone in my hand and asked if I had the logo sticker that came with the phone. I responded that I did not, but counter-questioned him as to why he was interested in having such a sticker. His answer was intriguing; he believed that if people saw the Apple logo on his scooter, they would automatically assume that he owned an iPhone. In his perspective, this served as a status symbol, signalling to others that he was financially well-off.

This incident is a clear illustration of how people can be uniquely unpredictable, displaying varied behaviours and perspectives towards different things. It's a reminder that everyone views the world through their own lens, assigning meanings and values to objects and symbols in a way that makes sense to them.

In the realm of business and life in general, understanding these diverse perspectives can be a real game-changer. The one who best understands their prospects or audiences, who can tap into these unique viewpoints and cater to them, ultimately comes out on top.

Magic of a quarter

Let me now introduce you to Yadav Garage, another workshop situated in Kalyan. It's owned by Avadhesh Yadav, referred to as Yadav from hereon, who left formal education after completing 8th grade and entered the automotive field in 2006. His wife and kids reside in his hometown, Uttar Pradesh. At Yadav Garage, there are six individuals working alongside him:

1. Sunil, Yadav's nephew, doesn't draw a salary.

2. Guddu, Chotu, and Niraj are all around 16 years old and without a high school diploma, and each gets an average salary of ₹6,000 per month.

3. Jaydeep, who holds a B.Com. degree and draws ₹7,500 in salary per month.

4. Vakil, who operates the denting and painting unit separately, pays a commission for each car.

5. Ajju, along with his assistant Aslam, manages the AC unit under the name Ajju AC Service. Unlike Vakil, Ajju pays a monthly rent of ₹4000 to Yadav, so no commission is involved.

6. Arun, Yadav's younger brother, serves as the second-in-command at the garage.

In addition to their salaries, all these individuals, except Guddu, Ajju, and Aslam, live together, and Yadav covers their living expenses.

I captured the above photo while standing inside Yadav Garage, facing the entrance. Behind me is a storage room, followed by an open area that Yadav utilises for parking cars that will be in the garage for more than one day. Below is a photo of the storage space, which serves as the area where they keep their parts, tools, compressor, car keys, used parts, and anything else that doesn't belong in the passage is dumped there, as clearly visible.

As dirty or unorganised as you might find it, this is how most garages in India function - there's often a lack of organisation, with things scattered and no proper system in place. The photo depicts this reality well, showing cluttered spaces and items just lying around. Additionally, the entire structure is illegal, and the open space used for parking cars with major repairs isn't even part of the rented premise.

Storage space at Yadav Garage.

You might assume that a garage's operations revolve around tools, cleaning cloths, uniforms, and chai breaks twice a day. That's true, however, the most essential fuel for nearly all garages across the country, akin to protein powder in the words of mechanics, is Vimal. Those who consume it will do it, rain or shine, in health or sickness.

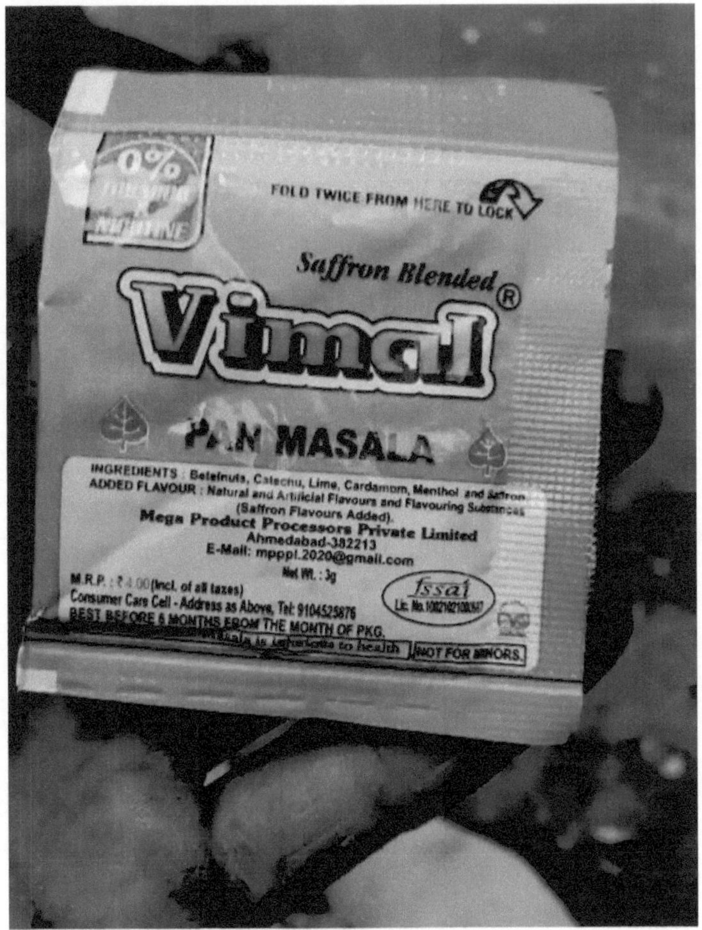

Picture credits: Anar

Garages in India are of different sizes, starting with those run by just one person, who then hires a helper after experiencing decent demand and growth. Gradually, they employ more mechanics to meet increasing demand and expand their operations. Eventually, they may begin to hire non-mechanic staff like an advisor cum manager and an accountant. Some garages follow this transition, while others may jump directly to the third or fourth category from the start. However, some garages remain solo or with a helper for their entire existence.

Yadav Garage falls into the third category and is highly popular in Kalyan. It handles an average of 7 cars per day, with numbers reaching 12-15 on good days, which is comparable to larger garages. The first three categories of garages often have a shady appearance, like Yadav's, but this actually works to their advantage as customers perceive them as budget-friendly options. The fourth category is also the one that invests in infrastructure and typically provides GST bills as an option for customers, has a branded uniform for all employees, etc.

First category	Solo mechanic
Second category	+ a helper
Third category	+ more mechanics, poor infra
Fourth category	+ more mechanics & non technical staff with focus on infra. Also has GST.

In many third and fourth category garages, you'll often come across some distinct personalities. There's usually a very talkative individual who enjoys chatting about anything except cars. They always seem to have a story for every topic, and sometimes they use unrelated examples to explain car problems or persuade you about something. In every garage, you'll find the "ustaad" mechanic, who's like the top-ranked expert. With years of experience and a proven track record, they're the go-to person for other mechanics when they need help. The ustaad mechanic can often diagnose car problems just by driving the car or even by hearing a description of the symptoms with pretty good accuracy. Then, you'll likely find a mischievous young chap in the garage, always sporting a smile. This lively character works for a low salary with little to no experience, takes care of small tasks for the garage owner, and enjoys sharing jokes with the seniors. Additionally, there's usually a highly egoistic individual who prefers to keep to themselves and doesn't talk much with others. Despite their reserved nature, they efficiently get the work done without causing much fuss. Another common character is the punctual worker who consistently arrives on time and prefers to leave promptly, unless there's an urgent situation requiring their attention. While not present in every garage, some may also have at least one individual with a criminal history, often having served time in jail, typically for serious offences like attempted murder.

Like any other business, garages also incur recurring costs to keep the shop running. Rent is one of the primary expenses. Starting with the rent, it tends to be relatively low, especially for garages falling into the first three categories. However, the exact amount depends on the location. For example, Yadav pays only ₹16,000 per month for the entire area, which is quite affordable. In many cases, landlords may not formalise rental agreements, particularly when the property is jointly owned by multiple family members. This informal arrangement can lead to complications, such as difficulties in reclaiming security deposits. Such situations are more common in Tier 3 cities and beyond. A garage also typically employs denters and polishers full-time. Painters, AC technicians, and electricians often freelance across various garages. But if a garage frequently needs these services, it may hire a full-time expert in each area. The salary structure varies significantly across different garage categories. For instance, younger employees, typically below 20 years old, often earn less than ₹10,000. In contrast, at garages like Yadav's, where living expenses are covered by the owner and most employees are part of the family, salaries may be lower. In other garages, especially those in the fourth category, salaries are higher. The most senior mechanics may earn around ₹25,000, mid-senior mechanics about ₹18,000, denters around ₹15,000, polishers around ₹9,000, and advisors between ₹20,000 and ₹25,000. An advisor's salary may also depend on additional factors, such as bringing in customers from previous workplaces or handling insurance claims, which can increase their value to the garage. In third-party garages, the typical monthly salary routine differs from what you might expect in other workplaces. Instead of receiving their full salaries in the first week of the month, employees often approach the owner multiple times before the salary due date, requesting small advances due to urgent financial needs. The owner may sometimes refuse these requests but often provides advances ranging from ₹500 to ₹1000, depending on the perceived legitimacy of the need and the relationship with the employee. When the actual salary payment is due, the owner may occasionally delay it, and employees, having received advances earlier, may not protest much. Managing the workers in the garage is an extremely difficult job, and the owner has to be very careful at all times. Operating a garage entails various costs beyond just rent and salaries. Electricity bills are a constant expense. Additionally, there's the "mess-up" cost—inevitable in any garage due to the nature of the work. When something is inadvertently damaged or lost, especially if it's easily noticeable, like a car key, the garage must bear the cost of replacement. However, if the damage or loss is less conspicuous, it may go unnoticed, with the assumption that the owner won't discover it. Additionally, providing chai (tea) for the staff can add up, with a garage accommodating 10 to 15 people spending around ₹8000 to ₹10000 per month on chai alone. Water expenses typically amount to ₹40 per drum, with approximately 24 drums used monthly. Furthermore, garages must maintain inventories of tools, parts, compounds, oils, coolants, and AC gas, among other necessities for technicians. Disposal of scrap materials, such as old car parts, also incurs a monthly fee of approximately ₹800 to ₹1000 for trash collection services to the guys from the local municipal corporation, who charge the fee mainly to pick it up and dump it in their trash truck. Moreover, garages often encounter bad debt situations where they receive partial or no payment from certain customers, adding to their financial challenges.

Credit plays a crucial role in the survival of most garages. When generating bills for customers, a significant portion typically comprises the cost of parts, with the remainder covering labour charges. For example, if a bill amounts to ₹10,000, with ₹2500 attributed to labour and ₹7500 to parts, the garage will receive the entire payment from the customer upfront. However, the garage will then need to settle its dues with the local parts vendor, usually within a month. In the interim, the garage utilises the total bill amount to cover its operating expenses. This reliance on credit allows garages to maintain cash flow while fulfilling customer orders promptly. The credit terms offered by a parts vendor to a garage depend on the payment history and behaviour of the garage owner over time. Positive payment behaviour is gradually rewarded as trust is built, often resulting in extended credit periods, and the part vendor, when required, spends more effort sourcing something for the garage. Conversely, irresponsible or delayed payments can quickly tarnish the garage's reputation, making vendors cautious about extending credit. In essence, the garage effectively receives an interest-free loan from the parts vendor, allowing it to manage cash flow more effectively. Any application that seeks to bypass garages and directly sell parts to customers disrupts the established financial cycle of the garage. This disruption undermines the incentive for garages to actively seek customers through such apps. As a result, these apps may end up serving merely as supplementary tools for garages, becoming the source of "fill in the blanks" rather than being integral to customer acquisition. Moreover, when such apps introduce commissions and weekly payment releases, the situation worsens for garages, as it further erodes their control over the customer relationship and financial flow.

In the third and fourth categories, a typical garage services around 2000 cars per year, including both minor and major repairs. Interestingly, many of these car services result in losses for the garage, while some break even, and a portion yield profits substantial enough to offset the losses and generate a decent overall profit. Such garages can expect annual revenues ranging from ₹60,00,000 to ₹1,15,00,000, including both parts and labour charges. It's important to note that this figure represents revenue, and after deducting operating costs, the actual profit typically ranges from ₹1,50,000 to ₹5,00,000 per month. However, there are exceptions, such as larger setups offering additional in-house services like wheel alignment, tire sales, etc., which can achieve annual revenues of 3–4 crores. Nevertheless, the calculation provided here is reflective of the financial dynamics prevalent in most third- and fourth-category garages across India. You can determine the revenue category of a garage by observing how many cars they have for denting and painting at any given time, as well as how many staff members are dedicated to this department. Garages often prioritise denting and painting because it's relatively easy to satisfy customers quickly, with noticeable before-and-after effects that make car owners happy. Additionally, there's significant profit potential, as margins per panel are typically high, and the work can be completed relatively quickly with less chaos compared to other services.

For example, the cost of an overcoat (painting the entire car) on a typical hatchback can range from ₹25,000 for average-quality work to ₹1,50,000 at a larger workshop. A garage charging a decent rate, say between ₹30,000 and ₹45,000, can make a profit of at least ₹15,000 to ₹20,000 on each job. Therefore, if you consistently see a garage full of cars awaiting denting and painting, you can infer that they generate good revenue from these services.

Service is a significant reason for many cars to visit the garage at a defined interval. Even if the driver thinks the car is fine, a detailed diagnosis by the mechanic often reveals two or three underlying issues.

Common examples include brake pads, brake cylinders, disc skimming, wiper blades, indicator bulbs, and drive belts. In addition to the labour charges for the service itself, garages can generate additional income with minimal effort by replacing these parts during a routine service.

Typically, labour charges for a periodic service at any garage for a hatchback range from ₹800 to ₹2500. The lower end of this spectrum may not include a car wash, while the higher end is likely to include one. The labour involved in a service typically includes draining old engine oil and refilling it, topping up or replacing coolant as needed, checking and cleaning spark plugs, cleaning air and AC filters, inspecting and cleaning brake pads for the front tires and brake liners for the rear tires, and checking the brake oil level. Additionally, some larger garages that charge higher labour rates may also inspect the battery, lubricate all door hinges with grease, and perform an ECU scan to address any warning lights present, providing photos as evidence.

As for parts, every service generally includes an oil filter, which can range from ₹95 for Maruti Suzuki cars to ₹500 for other mass-market cars. Air filters and AC filters are typically replaced, with prices starting at ₹260 for the former and ₹450 for the latter and going up to ₹1000 and ₹2000, respectively. Most garages, regardless of volume, maintain a margin of at least 4% on the original parts sold at MRP. When it comes to engine oil, many manufacturers recommend the 5W30 for a wide range of cars. However, garages often overlook this recommendation because not all cars require 5W30, especially some mass-market models. Additionally, there's a significant information gap between fully synthetic and semi-synthetic engine oils. Most garages struggle to explain the concrete differences between them and usually just suggest that fully synthetic is better. Customers often opt for fully synthetic oil out of a fear of missing out and a desire to do what's best for their car, reasoning that the price difference of ₹1000 or ₹2000 won't make much of a difference in the long run. (You know, like, "acha wala dalenge, ₹1000 ya ₹2000 ka farak se kya hi hoga.")

For most petrol hatchbacks and sedans, the engine oil consumption is around 3.5 litres. Well-known oil companies typically sell semi-synthetic oil starting at ₹1550 onwards for a 3.5-liter can, while fully synthetic oil starts at ₹2200 onwards for the same quantity. Garages can make a profit of at least ₹300 per oil can from a well-known company when purchased individually, with profits increasing as the quantity rises. For instance, a barrel of low-quality 225-litre oil may cost around ₹45,000, which translates to ₹200 per litre. For any reputable brand's semi-synthetic and fully synthetic oils, barrels may cost ₹60,000 and ₹90,000, respectively. Regardless of the brand and grade of oil, all barrels yield a minimum of double profit for garages.

This is because garages typically sell fully synthetic oil for ₹700 to ₹800 per litre. Moreover, buying several oil cans together often secures better rates than purchasing single pieces. It's important to note that the pricing examples mentioned depend on the specific brand and grade of oil. I specified "well-known" brands because many smaller brands may sell for significantly cheaper, sometimes as low as 50% of the price of a well-known brand, as an incentive to boost sales. Sometimes garages engage in scams where they offer attractively low labour charges to lure customers in, only to compensate by using very low-quality oil and charging the same amount as a reputable brand. For example, there's a brand called Kasaul, and when you inquire over the phone about the oil brand the mechanic will use, they might pronounce it in a way that sounds like Castrol, a well-known brand. Customers, thinking they're getting Castrol oil, are pleased and often never find out if it was actually Kasaul or Castrol. Even if they do find out, the mechanic may insist they mentioned Kasaul, not Castrol, shifting the blame onto the customer's hearing.

For reference, if a single can of Castrol oil costs the garage ₹1800, Kasaul might cost them only ₹800 to ₹1000, a significant difference. So, if you think you're getting a hefty discount on labour charges, be aware that the garage might recoup those savings from your pocket in other ways. Additionally, oil cans often contain a coupon code under the cap that can be redeemed for cashback. This is mainly intended for the mechanic or garage to use, but in many cases, the garage owner opts to give it to the mechanic as a form of incentive or tip. For your reference, I have summarised the service estimate for a Hyundai Venue at a third-party garage with all original parts:

- 5w30 fully synthetic oil, 3.5 litres: ₹2400

- Oil filter: ₹150

- Air filter: ₹350

- AC filter: ₹480

- Grease: ₹75

- Coolant 1L: ₹314

- Cleaning cloth: ₹20

- Wash: ₹300

- Service labour: ₹1200

Total: ₹5289

In comparison, bigger, more sophisticated garages typically don't break down costs for wash, grease, and cloth separately. Instead, they charge a consumable fee of approximately ₹400 and may also include wiper water fluid, etc. These garages often sell service packages and differentiate between various checkpoints for the car. However, some view this as unnecessary and a gimmick to increase profits by bloating the service with additional, sometimes trivial, checkpoints. For example, checking the AC may simply involve turning it on and feeling if it's cold enough, while checking bulbs may be counted as separate points for each bulb. Additionally, including a trial drive as a checkpoint may be viewed as shady and an attempt to inflate the service list. In my opinion, the essential services required at yearly intervals, or every 10,000 or 15,000 kilometres, depending on the car, include oil and oil filter changes, replacing air and AC filters if they appear very dirty, brake service involving cleaning brake pads and liners, and wheel alignment and balancing. These are the fundamental maintenance tasks that every car needs, regardless of how they're categorised into packages. Other checks can be done as needed, and you can always communicate specific problems to the mechanic for attention.

The bill provided might seem a bit unrealistic, especially for Venue owners, because such bills typically arise only during the first two oil change services. Wear and tear usually becomes more noticeable after the third service, or 30,000 kilometres, leading to additional repairs as the car ages. It's worth noting that bills of similar amounts are possible even at dealerships, which I'll discuss in the next chapter. In the first three categories, most garages outsource washing, leaving wheel alignment and balancing as another service often not fulfilled by the garage itself. Here are the typical prices at any tire store:

- Wheel alignment: ₹250 to ₹550

- Wheel balancing: ₹70 to ₹120 per tire

- Balancing weights: ₹2 to ₹6 per gram (average weight around 150 grams)

- Rotation: ₹50 per tire

Rotation can usually be done for free if requested, as the garage typically removes all tires for brake service anyway. It's worth mentioning that many people prioritise cosmetic services over essential ones like wheel alignment and balancing to save money, even though the latter is crucial for vehicle safety. Despite this, a garage can earn around ₹1500 in labour and a 4% margin on all original parts, totaling around ₹2051 for a job that typically takes 1 to 3 hours. Service is often seen as quick money for garages and a way to build rapport with customers for future work, where the real money lies. Disc skimming is another service that can yield close to a 100% margin for garages. Drivers often categorise car repairs based on urgency. Breakdowns are addressed immediately, followed by jobs like clutch changes or minor denting and painting, which are scheduled at a convenient time. Minor repairs with minimal impact on daily driving are often deferred until the next periodic service.

Let me tell you a secret: performing a periodic service is a straightforward job, so there's no need to be picky about which garage you choose. If you're someone who enjoys DIY projects and can follow a simple

YouTube video, you can easily do a periodic service yourself. It's that simple and doesn't require any special expertise. The real expertise comes into play when diagnosing other problems in the car. A novice or inexperienced mechanic might try various solutions to diagnose a problem, while a highly experienced one will quickly narrow down the possibilities and pinpoint the exact issue. This level of expertise only comes with years of practice and repairing thousands of cars. In fact, if you have a mechanic's phone number, you could call them for your next service, and many would be willing to come to your doorstep for as little as ₹500-₹600. Although there are many mechanics with high integrity, this kind of arrangement often happens behind the garage owner's back.

People often don't appreciate when a garage solves a problem quickly, which is often the result of years of practice and hard work. This is one reason why garages may prefer to take their time with repairs, as they can charge more or the right price if they keep the car parked for a couple of hours, solve the problem, and then return it. This tendency is especially true with wiremen. For instance, if a car's key is not detected and the car won't start, the garage may ask you to tow the vehicle to the garage for repair. However, in many cases, the issue may be a simple key-matching problem that can be fixed on the spot in just five minutes without opening anything or using any tools. You can easily find tutorials on YouTube by searching for "key matching for <car name>." The market rate for this service is around ₹1500, but if the garage does it in front of the car owner, they may face pushback on the cost, as people may feel it's unfair to charge for such a quick fix. This can lead to negotiations and potentially leave the wireman feeling regretful about offering the service. Wiremen and AC technicians, as I mentioned earlier, primarily work on contract across multiple workshops but rarely receive direct customer calls. This is because people prefer to have a sense of assurance about whom to contact when things go wrong. This preference is also one of the reasons why mobile mechanics have struggled to gain traction in India. Additionally, some individuals are hesitant to shop online for the same reason: they want the reassurance of a physical location and established reputation. Online purchases in India are primarily for accessories, with browsing for tires and batteries mainly done for price comparison when buying from a physical store. However, all tire companies have implemented limits on the discounts that shops can offer to maintain fair pricing across the area. If one tire shop sells a tire at a significantly lower price than the market rate, other shops can notify the manufacturer, who may issue warnings or even withdraw from the dealership after multiple complaints. Despite these regulations, tire shops often manage to sell at lower rates while staying under the company's radar. Similarly, bigger garages have numerous rules and regulations, along with established processes, but often fail to implement them effectively. Interestingly, the price limits set for offline retail do not apply to online marketplaces like Amazon or Flipkart, allowing for greater flexibility in pricing.

When you tell a tire shop that you've found better rates online, they'll often respond by raising concerns about the quality and warranty issues associated with online purchases. They'll create a fear of missing out (FOMO) by emphasising that if you buy from them, you'll have direct access to them for warranty claims and replacements. Even though they can't match the online rates, they instil the belief that paying a bit extra at their shop will be beneficial in the long run. Additionally, some prominent tire shops may offer to manually adjust the warranty terms, providing you with a new tire under warranty after 11 or 12 months. Others might go as far as asking you to find the cheapest rate in the market and guaranteeing a price below that. These tactics further reinforce the idea that buying from a physical store provides added value and peace of mind.

Batteries typically come with a 25- or 30-month guarantee, followed by an additional 25- or 30-month warranty. During the guarantee period, if a battery is identified as faulty, it will be replaced at no cost. However, the warranty period may not seem beneficial if you purchase the battery from an offline vendor. This is because the pricing they offer is often much lower than the manufacturer's suggested retail price (MRP), sometimes up to 50% lower. During the warranty period, you can claim a 20% instant rebate, but this rebate is calculated based on the MRP. For example, if a battery has an MRP of ₹100 and you purchase it for ₹48 directly from a battery shop (including a rebate for the old battery), the warranty discount will be calculated based on the MRP, meaning you would get the new battery under warranty for ₹80, excluding the rebate for the old battery. This setup doesn't make sense because you can purchase a new battery directly at a much lower rate and still receive a guarantee. As a result, many people only realise this discrepancy when their battery fails during the warranty period, leading to dissatisfaction.

Talking about online behaviour, car owners frequently turn to platforms like Boodmo to cross-check the pricing of parts they receive from garages. Garages themselves sometimes use Boodmo to send estimates, especially when they're experiencing delays from part vendors. However, for garages, the utility of Boodmo is limited to generating estimates. This is because the delivery of parts through Boodmo often takes a long time, and there's a risk of mismatched parts due to the wide variety of car models. Additionally, resolving issues with customer support can be a cumbersome process for garages, leading to delays and potential financial complications.

Let's bring back Rajesh, about whom I mentioned earlier in the "technological tax" scenario.

This time he is planning to go on a trip on Friday and intends to get his decade-old i20 serviced at a third-party workshop called Yadav Garage. Rajesh has previously visited this garage twice for his car's service. He calls Yadav and says, "Yadav bhai kaise ho? Main Chavan bolra hu, yaad aaya? Bohot pehle aaya tha i20 ke service ke liye, tumne mere gaadi ka suspension ka bhi kaam kiya tha." Yadav, although he doesn't remember who Rajesh is since the contact is not saved in his new phone, responds, "Ha maalik, boliye kya seva kar sakte hai aapki." To which Rajesh replies, "Arey gaadi ka servicing karna tha aur thode bohot chote mote problems bhi hai toh wo bhi thik karwana tha toh aaj abhi pick up kar paenge?" This conversation takes place on a Wednesday, late afternoon at around 4:00 pm, so Yadav insists that Rajesh pick up the car tomorrow morning, being Thursday, and Rajesh agrees. Rajesh then follows up at 8 p.m. for confirmation of his pickup after sending his home's location on WhatsApp, and Yadav confirms his pickup by 11 a.m. The next morning, Rajesh waits for Yadav's call but doesn't receive any communication. Finally, at 11 a.m., Rajesh decides to call Yadav, but Yadav doesn't pick up. Feeling upset, Rajesh plans to wait a little longer, hoping that Yadav will show up. After some time, Rajesh calls again and says, "Arey Yadav bhai, kya hua, aane wale the na aap? Phone bhi nahi uthare ho mera." To which Yadav responds, "Ha sorry sir, thoda kaam mein tha, mujhe thoda time dijiye, abhi tak ladka aaya nahi hai, jaise hi aaega main gaadi leleta hu." Rajesh replies, "Thike thoda jaldi karo, kaam aaj hi pura karna hai." Yadav acknowledges this and assures Rajesh that the work will be completed today itself. You see, this is the kind of expectation someone like Rajesh has from a garage. Even after confirming twice on the phone, he's still unsure if the pickup will happen on time. And this is for a garage where he personally knows the owner and has been there at least twice. It's almost 1:15 p.m. now, and Rajesh starts to feel a little frustrated. He calls again, saying, "Yadav bhai, yaar pick up karne wale ho ki nahi, ladka abhi tak nahi aaya kya?" Yadav responds, "Ladka toh aagaya hai lekin ek dusre kaam mein busy hai, bas 15 mins dedo, please main bhejta hu. Apna address kaha ka hai?" Rajesh, despite sending the address on WhatsApp last night, politely tells him, "Rambaug mein hai 6 number, aapko location bheja hai Whatsapp pe, Mhaskar hospital ke yaha pe aake phone karo." Now, even though Mhaskar Hospital is a very prominent landmark, the pickup guy may not know the exact address. Rajesh doesn't want to take any chances now, so he calls Yadav again exactly 15 minutes after the last call. "Ha, nikle kya ladke?" Rajesh asks. Yadav responds, "Ha, bas niklenge ek minute mein." But as expected, Yadav just made that up, as the boys were nowhere close to leaving for the pickup. The distance from Yadav's garage to Rambaug will take approximately 15 minutes, so Rajesh calls again after 30 minutes, this time very frustrated. "Yadav bhai, kya hai yaar ye? Main itna phone karra hu aapko aur aap mujhe har call pe pagal bana rahe ho. Gaadi ka kaam karna hai ki nahi?" Yadav replies, "Sorry, sir, wo ek customer aagaya tha, abhi nikal gaya hai. Banda aata hoga aapke pass ek 5 minutes mein."

Remember, Rajesh doesn't drive his car much, so he wouldn't know the current status of the puncture and battery in his car. Luckily, everything works well when the boys from Yadav arrive. But just imagine if it wasn't the case; then the pick-up would have been delayed by another hour at the minimum. Rajesh tells about some problems that he would like to be addressed by Yadav (customer note): the horn does not work properly, the brakes make noise, the car makes a rattling noise after shifting the car from 2nd to 3rd gear, the indicator is not working, the stick door patti is not properly fixed, and the radio antenna is broken. He also asks the pick-up boys to properly tune up the car. There are more problems present in the car that Rajesh does not know about, like the left wiper water nozzle is not working, the central lock is not working in the rear left door, and the blower mode doesn't change to leg only. Here is a crucial mistake that most, if not all, garages make: they do not write about any of these problems and remember only the top 2-3 crucial ones, depending on the customer to constantly bug them for the status of pending problems. Rajesh also wants to install a new infotainment screen but waits till the work is done to make sure he still has the budget to do so. The car then gets picked up successfully and is on its way to the garage. If you realise it, the pickup infrastructure at any third-party garage in the country is messed up. It is always delayed, as it's the mechanics who do the pick-up of the car once they get free from a car's work. There is mostly a single bike used for garage work, be it procuring parts, pick-up and drop, breakdown assistance, miscellaneous, etc. So, one has to wait until the bike arrives. For any pick-up, the mechanic will make 2-3 calls to the customer to ask for the address, as many garage personnel cannot use Google Maps. An average pick-up from a nearby location will take half an hour multiplied by two mechanics, which is an hour, as one will come back on the bike and the other will bring the car. Garages do not prioritise pickup reports, which capture the car's condition, especially cosmetic damages, to avoid liability for old damages. Many car owners are unaware of all the cosmetic damage to their vehicles. Dealerships invest considerable effort in managing inventory reports and documenting cosmetic damage to cars. However, most garages do not prioritize this task. Even if they have the skills, mechanics at garages are usually assigned to work on vehicles rather than handle administrative tasks like inventory reports. Additionally, mechanics may be reluctant to engage in tasks beyond vehicle maintenance. As a result, garages often overlook documenting cosmetic damages. In some cases, garages may be willing to compensate for minor damages to a small percentage of the cars they service, viewing it as an acceptable trade-off for their overall operations. Some more sophisticated garages attempt this step after the car has reached the workshop, which is an improvement over not doing it at all. Rajesh's car reaches the garage shortly after, and the two mechanics who picked it up start working on another car. It's 4 p.m., and Rajesh calls Yadav for an update, as it's been 2 hours since the pickup. Yadav responds, "Ha malik, abhi just lunch hua hai, abhi aapka hi gaadi le raha hoon." Rajesh confirms again, "Yadav bhai, aaj kaam hoga na? Kal subah mujhe Jalgaon jaana hai," and Yadav assures him that everything will be done. However, Rajesh still isn't convinced that everything will go smoothly. He decides to go to the garage himself to push Yadav to get the work done, see for himself the solutions in the car, and try to save money wherever he can. In the meantime, Yadav opens both front tires to ensure that if the customer comes, it won't appear as if nothing was done on the car at all. Rajesh arrives and asks about the status of the car, to which Yadav replies, "Gaadi khol diya hai, bas oil-paani leke aana hai. Abhi ladke dusre gaadi ka bas ek kaam khatam karde, unko bhejta hu." Now, there are two kinds of people: one who will always get the parts themselves in hope of saving money; even if they don't, they will know for a fact that they are not being charged more by the garage, so it then becomes a transparent affair; and the second kind, who are often inactive during the entire process and approve work as per their budget. While category one to category three garages are totally okay with people getting the parts themselves, category four garages normally hesitate here because they care about the spare part margin. So, you will often hear a common example where they jokingly ask you if you are allowed to take ingredients to a restaurant. This is also because the personas of customers can be largely different across categories. Rajesh, to accelerate the process, decides to get the parts himself after getting the list of things from Yadav, who also tells him the shop where he should get them. Rajesh procures the parts, and Yadav gets done with the periodic service without any need for replacement of the parts checked during the process, like brake pads, brake liners, disc rotors, etc. Rajesh then asks for the status of customer note jobs, to which Yadav says that he will check them now. Yadav cleans the choked-up wiper nozzle, which then starts working; Arun repairs the wiring for the left rear door; and Ajju tells Rajesh that he will have to replace the entire AC control module, which is expensive. Since Rajesh doesn't drive much, he can live without the leg-blower mode function, as most people keep it on the face anyway. So, all the problems get fixed under ₹500, and Rajesh is happy. Then comes Vakil, pointing at the various dents and scratches. He says, "Sir, gaadi mein bohot jyada scratch aur dent hai, acha nahi dikh raha hai aur paint bhi purana ho gaya hai. Repaint karane ka soche ho kya? Gaadi ekdum nayi ban jaegi. Wo dekho, aaj hi wo Ertiga ko pura paint kiya hai, lagri hai na ekdum new?" Rajesh asks for the cost. Now, even if Rajesh knows that he will not want to get it done, instead of a straight no, he chooses to ask the price so that everyone is happy since Vakil now might expect more business. Vakil replies, "Sir, jo kaam dealership waale ek laakh mein karenge, wohi main sirf ₹35,000 mein kar dunga, ekdum top quality aur jaha wo log aapko 10 din lagaenge, main sirf 5 din mein dunga." Now, every person has their own way of upselling the customer. One thing common in a lot of pitches is the demeaning of dealerships, which is a bad way to win a deal. Rajesh is now happy that everything got done at a very minimal rate. He finally plans to approve the infotainment for a whopping ₹12,500 with specifications of 6GB of RAM and 64GB of memory, this too from Yadav, who will source it from a wholesaler and retail it to Rajesh. You see, garages are everything for everyone. Just a matter of a few calls, and they will get everything you need for your car, provided they have the setup to do it, and they make money on it as well as provide support when required. What if someone gives competitive pricing with pan-India support for such things? That sounds like a big deal on the market. Rajesh approves the infotainment and leaves the garage for another job. At the same time, two cars come in for a minor instant repair, so Yadav places an order for the infotainment and shifts focus to the other cars.

By now, you should have realised that in third-party garages, you get highly prioritised if you are physically present there, as your presence acts like constant pressure on the garage staff to get the work done faster. It's just human behaviour, similar to how a student feels constant pressure when the teacher is present in the same room. It's 8 p.m., and Rajesh returns to the garage. He finds that the infotainment is nicely installed, checks it, and feels satisfied with the purchase. Now that all the major work on the vehicle is done,

Rajesh insists on a test drive to ensure everything is in proper order. However, as soon as he accelerates, he notices that there hasn't been much improvement in the pickup. He switches seats with Yadav so he can drive and check. As soon as Yadav gets on the driving seat, he says, "Rajesh bhai, iska toh clutch gaya hai, ekdum hard ho gaya hai." Rajesh replies, "Isliye tune-up nahi lag raha hai kya?" It turns out that by tuning up, he meant to improve the pickup, and Rajesh is used to the hard clutch, so he did not even realise that the clutch was faulty until Yadav pointed it out. To get a feel for a softer clutch, Yadav makes Rajesh sit in one of his customers' Tiago, and Rajesh finds a significant difference in the smoothness of its clutch pedal. Rajesh then asked for the solution and its cost from Yadav, who quoted ₹11,000 for the clutch plate, pressure plate, flywheel replacement, and labour. Rajesh, although he chose the wrong set of words to explain the pickup issue, got very upset that Yadav and the mechanics who picked up the car also did not report the problem to him. Yadav asked his mechanic why he didn't report it, and the driver thought the customer knew about the problem and didn't want to get it fixed since he mentioned three other problems in the car. Now, if you notice, due to the poor inspection, Rajesh thought there was no other work needed, so he spent money on the infotainment, which can't be returned, and now the whole budget is messed up because of this. If it were another person, they would have fought hard to return the infotainment, but Rajesh, in a frustrated manner, finally decides to spend more money to get the clutch assembly replaced. This kind of hierarchy mix-up happens frequently, and much of it could have been avoided simply by following the proper steps and not starting with the easiest tasks. Instead, every technician should begin with the most challenging job and then gradually move on to minor tasks, subject to the customer's approval and budget. In fact, in many automotive repairs, such as if the kilometres are not showing up on the instrument cluster, the most appropriate solution is to change the entire cluster. That's what most dealerships would do, but third-party workshops often have a repair mindset. They will first try four different solutions, each of which costs the customer money. If one of these solutions works, the customer is thrilled and saves a lot of money. However, if the only solution turns out to be replacing the part, then the customer has to bear the cost of the four unnecessary parts that were changed, in addition to the expense of the new part. When this happens, customers become extremely unhappy.

Upon Rajesh's request to replace the part, Yadav replied, "Malik abhi kaise hoga, 8:30 ho gaya hai abhi Saturday ko karenge kaam kyuki kal Friday band rahega." Friday is a weekly holiday for garages and most automotive shops. So Rajesh, being the polite man he is, requests Yadav to get the repair done tonight itself, as he had to leave for Jalgaon the next day for a family function. Yadav agrees and quickly starts making calls to the part vendors to somehow arrange the part, as it was already very late and arranging a clutch assembly for an old car like that at such short notice is tricky. Fortunately, the part arrives by 10:00 PM, much after all the parts shops and garages shut down. Rajesh plans to go to his house for dinner and come back as soon as possible to physically be there to supervise and constantly push the mechanics to get the work done at full speed. While everyone else leaves for home, Yadav and Arun start wrapping up the garage, parking all the cars inside their premises to then focus on Rajesh's car. Rajesh steps out after dinner, and on his way to the garage, he plans to buy a secret gift for Yadav and the boys. Remember how I mentioned that Vimal is a very crucial part of their tool stack? Similarly, there is one more thing that boosts the mechanic enough to get a day's worth of work done in a few hours, and that's the magic of a quarter. It's not like they cannot afford it; it's simply a gesture by Rajesh to thank them for working so late, as that's generally appreciated.

Every day, many people visit garages for car repairs, both minor and major. These garages often promise to return the cars at the requested time, but they sometimes take on more work than they can handle. They believe they can magically accommodate 10 cars into a space meant for 5 cars and still finish all of them on time, but this isn't possible given the workload and further dependency on spare parts availability. As a result, some customers end up waiting longer than expected, and many cars get delayed. This happens because garages find it hard to turn down business in order to attract new customers and make more money. Rajesh's experience highlights the challenges of getting a simple car service done, even when most things seem to go smoothly. Despite the availability of parts and quick work, the process can still be cumbersome. Yadav's cooperation and trustworthiness made things easier for

Rajesh, although he couldn't verify all of Yadav's repair recommendations. In a third-party garage, customers often encounter a lack of updates, approval processes, cost estimations, documentation like photos, reminders, or punctual delivery. When you arrive at the garage, you might find yourself waiting for assistance because everyone is occupied with other tasks. There's a tendency to oversell services, and customers may worry about the security of their car parts while in the garage. To ensure timely service, customers often need to be physically present and actively follow up with the mechanics. Unfortunately, important customer notes or small but crucial jobs are sometimes overlooked. Many customers simply agree with whatever the garage suggests without fully understanding the situation. Moreover, some garages may engage in deceptive practices, such as recommending unnecessary part replacements to increase their labor and spare part margins, even when a simple repair would suffice. In some garages, they may check your oil and decide not to change it if your car hasn't been driven much, despite still charging you for the service. Additionally, they may ask you to obtain a list of parts, only to return some of them to the supplier after charging you for the entire list. Unfortunately, some garages might even misuse your car for personal use by claiming it as a trial drive. Pricing strategies vary among garages, with some adjusting prices based on individual customers. For example, if a customer negotiated a significant discount in the past, the garage might increase prices to offset previous losses, potentially earning more than if the customer had paid full price initially. Interestingly, while both a Mahindra Scorpio and a BMW X5 may require similar amounts of paint and labour for painting, their pricing for this service can differ significantly. Additionally, if a technician notices work done by another garage, they may inquire about the price and claim they could have done the same job for much less. However, this claim is that they would have charged much less for the same work. However, this assertion may not hold true because they know you've already had the work done and are unlikely to repeat it, regardless of the lower labor costs they might offer. In fact, it's common for every garage to attribute any issues to the previous garage's work. Despite this, many people still choose to go to third-party garages. The main reasons are the lower cost and the ability to customise services. The "bhai ye karde na yaar" attitude is prevalent in garages, and mechanics often don't mind doing small tasks for free. However, there are only a few sophisticated garages that send reminders and photos of the work done. Unfortunately, these photos often lack context, making them somewhat pointless for the customer.

Rajesh's work is completed by 2 a.m., and negotiations begin. Unfortunately, discounts are often negotiated unfairly for garages. Customers who have already negotiated before approving the job sometimes try to further reduce the price after the work is done. Garages sometimes agree with the customer's demands on their first visit to make them happier and ensure their return. Despite the poor treatment, garages often have high retention rates. For example, in Rajesh's case, if he encounters any issues with the clutch in the following weeks, he may be upset but will likely return to Yadav Garage. He expects some form of customer support from them, and if Yadav Garage can provide a satisfactory solution, Rajesh will be happy again and continue using their services. This kind of customer loyalty rarely occurs with applications, as the entire support process is typically handled offline by the customer. Rajesh pays the full amount and heads home. His scenario was relatively simple, focusing on straightforward work. However, the situation becomes much more complicated for cars that take longer to repair. In such cases, there may be no updates provided, requiring the customer to visit the workshop daily. Additionally, there may be a lack of proper diagnostics, and many parts may not be readily available. Even when parts are available, customers may not have the budget for them. As a result, repairs are often delayed for various reasons. You may even find some cars parked in the garage indefinitely because the customer couldn't afford the repairs. Garages hate to deal with illiterate people who do not understand anything and only feel they are always being cheated by charging more, so squeeze the garage owner while negotiating. Some people also say things like "aaj ₹8000 kar deta hu baaki mera salary 2 din mein aaega tab kar dunga pakka." Now, you might feel the garage will not release the car in this scenario, but not all do that. They have no option but to go according to the customer and follow up constantly every few days, and some eventually turn out to be bad debts. Not just that, there are also some people who bring vehicles that appear to be used by government officials on duty; they will get work done for ₹5000 but have the workshop generate a bill for ₹20,000, which will be then sent for reimbursement so they make money on that. Garages also feel very comfortable with someone from the same native place as them and don't hesitate to do more for them, provided it's a win-win for both, whereas garages and automotive shops don't like it much when there is a third party representing the owner, which in most cases is the driver. That's because it is immensely difficult to upsell anything to them. A lot of sophisticated garages with GST numbers also tend to play with their billing; they generate the pro forma invoice for the customer's reference, and if the customer wants to pay in cash and does not have the final invoice, then the garage will generate the tax invoice with a much lesser value compared to the original work. For example, if there's a proforma generated for ₹26,750 that the car owner pays in cash, then the garage will generate the tax invoice only for say ₹9000, but if the same customer wanted a GST bill, then the garage would have no option but to create the exact same tax invoice and give a copy to the customer without hampering it.

A mechanic usually divides their salary into expenses like rent, food (rashan), and miscellaneous items and sends the remaining amount to their family back in the village or native place. Mechanics often spend a significant portion of their earnings on tobacco and alcohol. Many of them are not practical when it comes to family planning, marrying early, and having too many children without planning for the financial implications. Despite these challenges, they somehow manage to keep their families happy. There's also a mechanic I know who dresses in formal attire every morning before heading to the garage, where he switches to his mechanic uniform. He does this to make his kids and the community believe that he works in an office, in a white-collar job. Most mechanics don't have medical insurance but somehow manage to arrange money when someone in the immediate family needs medical treatment. The salary structure, as I mentioned before, is divided into multiple parts over the month, which makes it difficult for mechanics to save any money.

I discussed the concept of technological tax earlier in this book, and to add to that, not all garages prioritise productivity. They are reluctant to upgrade themselves or adopt technology to improve customer service. For them, everything in that regard is "magajmaari" (meaning: a waste of time). They are hesitant to share commissions and lag behind in terms of technology. Even if they can use an app, their hands are always dirty from working on cars. So, how do you convince them to prioritise your feature-loaded app designed to simplify and improve their lives? It's a very challenging task to achieve at scale. In fact, if you message any garage with a WhatsApp Business account, you'll often receive a default automated reply stating that they are unavailable and will respond as soon as possible, which is detrimental to the customer experience. The only aspect that sophisticated garages have begun to care about, thanks to fierce competition, is their Google ratings. This helps them attract tech-savvy, busy professionals who rely on Google searches to choose a garage. One thing I don't like about the garages is that a lot of them have this "meherbaani" attitude where they talk to you as if they are doing you a favour by not fooling you. This normally happens during negotiation, where they go like, "Main chahta toh aapko pura panel ka charge karta lekin aap special ho isliye aapke liye itne mein hi kar diya." It is absolutely nonsense and a ticket to make someone like me disappointed.

Fancy wrapper

Let me spoil the suspense for you: most mass-market dealerships are equally chaotic as a third-party garage, but they know how to present everything in a much better format. Customers normally hesitate to visit a third-party garage because they fear their car's work will not be done properly, proper parts may not be used, parts might get stolen, and they believe that such garages lack proper technique and equipment. They believe nothing of this sort will happen in the dealership as it is a brand. For dealerships, retention is a limited-period gift, as a car usually has a 3-year warranty or up to 1,50,000 km, whichever is earlier. So, by default, people go to the dealership during this term. But what is the dealer's measure to decide if the car is under warranty or not? They check their system to ensure the car has been serviced on time from any authorised service centre across the country until the warranty period exists. That means even if you get a service done outside, you can mostly still keep the warranty by again getting a service done from the dealership, as they have no way to know that you already got it done from a third-party garage; it is all about the records in their system. Some dealerships also recover the lapsed warranty for you if you also bought the car from them; they will not even try if you bought your car from a different dealership. Now, after the car purchase, there are typically three free services, whereas some brands only limit it to two. The first free service is after a month or 1000 km, whichever comes earlier. During this service, they are supposed to run an ECU scan, check the oil level, and top up fluids if required, such as transaxle oil, coolant, brake fluid, battery electrolyte, and windshield washer fluid. They also check fuel lines for leakages, clean condenser fins, and wash the car, according to most owner manuals. The second free service, which occurs after 6 months or 7000 km for a lot of cars, includes similar procedures. Please note that henceforth, wherever I mention X years or X km, it will mean whichever occurs earlier by default. The common thing between the first two services is that they are free, which means the owner should not be paying money for anything unless there is cosmetic damage that the owner wants to get fixed or something that is not covered under warranty, which then gets categorised as additional repair. I've never seen customers receive these complimentary services without being charged. Dealerships often include consumables like windshield washer fluid in the bill, ranging from ₹700 to ₹1100, which is an unethical practice. However, if you clarify upfront that you don't want to be charged for these items, there's a high chance the bill will be zero. The third service, being a free one, typically excludes labour charges and only includes the cost of parts. Usually, only the oil and oil filter need changing, totaling around ₹2,500 to ₹3000, excluding wheel alignment and balancing. Despite this, many people end up paying ₹7000 to ₹8000 for the same service at mass-market dealerships. Before I explain why, let me give you some average numbers regarding the scale at a mass-market dealership (such as Tata, Hyundai, or Maruti Suzuki). The daily intake averages 50 cars, which shoots up to 70 or even 80 sometimes on Saturdays and Sundays, with most of the cars coming in for free service. Mondays and Thursdays usually have the lowest intake. Most workshops in Tier 1 and Tier 2 cities work only on appointments; they will not entertain people who do not have an appointment. They will take the car but start the work only after the pending cars are done, so they deliver the next day compared to the same day for appointment cars. In these kinds of workshops that only work on appointments, the show-up rate is extremely high. Whereas in many Tier 3 workshops, despite the appointment structure being in place and people booking an appointment, there are more people who simply go without an appointment, and the workshop is used to that process. So, if there are 50 cars going into a workshop in a Tier 3 city, then only 18–20 out of them will have booked an appointment, with a no-show rate of 20%. Out of those who schedule an appointment, about 50% will opt for a pick-up from the dealership. This number depends on whether a dealership is charging for pickup and drop or not. Many of them charge a fee of ₹250 to ₹350 to cover the cost of their driver's travel to the customer's location. This also helps them filter out some people who don't want to pay for it, so they will drive it themselves. These are also the people who are hard to get approval from and ask too many questions, which typically limits the revenue from such users' pockets. As a side outcome, it also helps them keep their pick-up bandwidth up to par. Many dealerships offer free pickup services due to the high volume of customers they handle daily. When their pickup service reaches its capacity for the day, they may offer free pickup to customers willing to delay their service by a day. This helps smooth out daily operations, especially when dealing with walk-in customers. Additionally, if there's a competing workshop of the same company nearby that charges for pickup, offering a free pickup can attract customers. Dealerships prefer remote interactions with car owners because it's easier to get approvals over the phone. When customers are physically present, they tend to ask numerous questions, constantly seek advice from the advisor, feel pressure for quicker service, and may not approve all recommended work after a visual inspection. Remote interactions are faster, and customers typically trust the advisor's recommendations without applying pressure. The number of people opting for pick-up increases significantly when the charge is waived, indicating that even owners of expensive cars worth 15 or 30 lakh rupees mind paying a small fee for convenience. It's surprising, but true. Initially, most customer communication is handled by the Customer Relationship Executive (CRE) team until customers establish a rapport with an advisor. Due to high turnover among advisors at mass-market dealerships, rapport may not always develop, and advisors may delegate tasks like booking appointments to others, such as the receptionist. The CRE team's main responsibility is to drive sales, making them pivotal in dealership operations. Their responsibilities include a wide range of tasks, including managing reminders and follow-ups, selling insurance and extended warranties, ensuring monthly sales targets are met, re-engaging with lost customers, and attracting new customers from competitors. The team mainly comprises female staff, as their clientele primarily consists of men. When females make calls, customers are less likely to speak rudely or express dissatisfaction, resulting in more concise and to-the-point interactions. Their workflow relies heavily on Excel and the

Dealership Management System (DMS), which provides a list of customers to call based on their purchase date, although this data is most often limited to cars sold by their dealership. Furthermore, their manager often provides data obtained unethically from competitor dealerships. This data typically includes the name, model, last service date, location of the last service, kilometres at the last service, and VIN (Vehicle Identification Number). Customer Relationship Executives (CREs) use the VIN to access specific car information in the Dealership Management System (DMS), such as AMC (Annual Maintenance Contract) status, body shop details, insurance information, and upcoming service predictions based on historical kilometres between services. CREs manually enter this data into spreadsheets provided by their manager to generate a targeted list of customers to contact and potentially poach. With aggressive targets for selling Extended Warranties (EWs), AMCs, and insurance policies, CREs are trained to pitch these products even when customers call to book appointments. They gauge politeness and engagement during calls, using the opportunity to upsell EWs after verifying the car's status. CREs are also responsible for tracking and improving the monthly intake of cars. If you want to become their favourite customer, buy all the things I mentioned above. If you negotiate, they will also offer to give you freebies like 10 free washes or a basic wax polish valid for one year along with the insurance, but the catch is that they know it is very unlikely for someone to come all the way to the workshop just for a free wash, so ask for a free alignment instead, and they will be fine with that too. Now, let's return to why some customers end up paying ₹7000–₹8000 instead of the expected ₹3000. Suresh gets a call from his nearest Tata dealership to remind him about his Tata car's third service, which is due. The dealership's reminder system typically begins contacting customers 1 to 3 months before the service is actually needed. Suresh takes the car himself, as this is the first major service, and he wants to see how it goes. Upon arrival, the security guard takes the car key and asks him to register his entry at the reception. The receptionist at most dealerships will be a lady who will ask for the vehicle number, confirm the name, and assign an advisor who will attend as soon as he gets free, typically within 15 to 30 minutes. Meanwhile, the customer will sit in the customer lounge, which is no less than a kitty party where unknown people gossip about the dealership with each other over free chai served by the pantry man. The principal dealership has set a time limit for customers to be attended upon arrival, mostly 15 minutes, but that is not tracked or followed at mass-market dealerships, especially in Tier 2 and Tier 3 cities. Additionally, dealerships also have restrictions on inventory, time it takes for the car to get on the ramp, time spent on the ramp, total time for a service, etc.

Advisor Kiran enters the customer lounge within 15 minutes and calls out "6091" to locate Suresh, who raises his hand, indicating he is the owner of the car with the number ending in 6091. Kiran smiles at him and says, "Aa jao sir." Both of them proceed to the car, where Kiran starts taking photos from every angle to create an inventory report, documenting the car's condition at the time of submission. While taking pictures, he also asks if there are any issues with the car. Since the car is new and the likelihood of problems is very low, Kiran doesn't spend much time inspecting it and takes Suresh to his desk for an estimation. This is where the fancy treatment comes into play: Kiran orders tea or coffee for the customer and, in the meantime, recommends and obtains approval for the estimation. Kiran pitches adding AC disinfectant, wheel balancing and alignment, brake service, deep interior cleaning, consumables, lubrication, and brake cleaner, generating an estimation of ₹8532. Suresh, not understanding much about these services, asks, "Kiran bhai ye sab karwana chahiye kya? Estimation toh bohot jyada hai." To this, Kiran replies, "Naya gaadi hai sir, karwaoge toh acha rahega. Sab toh karate hai baaki aapke upar hai." This statement instantly creates the sense that getting these services done is essential for car care because most people do it. Suresh approves everything except the interior cleaning, as he finds his car clean enough at the moment. During subsequent major services, when only an oil change is needed without additional repairs or customer notes, the advisor will inspect the entire car and insist, "Sir, ye part kharab hone wala hai toh abhi gaadi aayi hai toh abhi hi kara do kyuki fir next direct ek saal baad hi aaegi." Some advisors even suggest, "Arey sir, last time aapko wo part warranty mein karke diya tha na toh ab ye bhi karwalo," in a 'meherbani' tone, which feels shady. If your car is under warranty and you try to explain a perception-based problem, such as a sound or vibration, the advisor might not put in enough effort to investigate, often concluding with "aisa hi rehta hai." However, if your car is out of warranty, the advisor may take the issue more seriously and seek approval for replacements if necessary. Since it's Suresh's first major service, Kiran also encourages him to purchase the annual maintenance contract (AMC) for a certain amount, pushing him towards that option. AMC is valuable to dealerships as it ensures customer retention, and advisors are often incentivized to sell a certain number of AMC each month or get in the good books of their managers and the organisation. Moreover, an advisor is given a monthly labour target to achieve, ranging from ₹4 lakhs to ₹6 lakhs on average, depending on the volume of the dealership. They also need to sell 5 to 25 extended warranties, again depending on factors such as dealership size, seniority, and other variables. While these targets are not unrealistic, they often force advisors to oversell or mislead their customers, leading to an unethical work culture throughout the organisation. Advisors are skilled at spotting signals; as you navigate through the dealership, they try to glean more information about you to tailor their sales approach. For instance, a customer who appears knowledgeable about cars will not be offered additional repairs that are unnecessary. They will identify customers who won't ask too many questions, those who seek discounts, those who are meticulous and caring about their cars, those who are sophisticated and don't seek discounts, those who lack car knowledge, those who hesitate to spend money on their car, those with angry behaviour, those who are patient and polite, and so on, and they will adapt their sales tactics accordingly.

Kiran creates a job card after approval and hands it over to the floor manager, who supervises and coordinates the tasks assigned to each technician. The floor manager allocates and supervises the mechanics, who report any additional repairs found directly to the advisor. Unlike garages, where everyone handles multiple tasks, dealerships are organised into departments, each with its own manager reporting to the general manager, who in turn reports to the VP of the dealership. Dealerships have implemented various processes that are not typically found in third-party workshops, such as service reminders, photo documentation, centralised services, and written documentation for all transactions. Most floor managers in dealerships are highly responsible and adept at managing multiple cars and staff members simultaneously, even under pressure. However, if you encounter a lazy or inefficient advisor, your experience can be frustrating. You may need to constantly chase them, making multiple calls a day just to ensure they fulfil their responsibilities. Poor communication leads to delays in updates, estimates, photo documentation, reminders, and delivery, ultimately resulting in a dissatisfactory experience for customers. The quality of the dealership experience also depends on the advisor-to-car ratio, ensuring that advisors aren't overwhelmed with too many cars, which can lead to some customers having a bad experience. Similar to third-party garages, advisors at dealerships also sometimes promise unrealistic delivery times to all customers. Customers who are present during the service often believe that being there will result in a lower bill. As mentioned earlier, even at a dealership, having a loud and rude attitude can sometimes result in prioritisation as the staff aims to get rid of you quickly. A key difference between third-party garages and dealerships is that the former offer customization, whereas the latter emphasise standardisation. Customers commonly express dissatisfaction due to issues such as poor washing, delivery delays, faulty workmanship, suspected overcharging, or damage occurring while the car is in the workshop. In such cases, customers typically approach the advisor first, and if the issue persists, they escalate it to the general manager, who you can also consider the chief grievance officer. Dealerships usually offer to redo any work that is found to be unsatisfactory. However, when customers claim that something broke or a new problem arose while the car was at the dealership, it can be a challenging situation for the general manager. While some claims may be legitimate, others may be attempts to scam the dealership for free replacements. Unfortunately, I've noticed that many dealerships don't take action on customer feedback, even after multiple instances. Dealerships are cautious about customers contacting the principal company's customer support, so they often go to great lengths to prevent this. If you have a legitimate concern, simply mentioning the possibility of sending an email to the company's customer support team may prompt the dealership to resolve the issue promptly, as ultimately, it's the dealership that will address the problem, regardless of whether an email is sent.

Some advisors engage in shady and unethical practices within the dealership. For instance, if a customer is hesitant to proceed with costly repairs due to budget constraints, the advisor may provide their alternate contact number and suggest contacting them later. Subsequently, the advisor may offer to conduct the same repairs at the customer's location for a much lower price, arranging for the necessary parts and bringing along a mechanic to divide the profits. This scenario is not uncommon, even in larger and more sophisticated workshops. In another instance, advisors may obtain approval for necessary repairs within the workshop but only register a basic service on the dealership's system. As a result, the tax invoice reflects a minimal amount, such as ₹4000, despite the actual work being worth ₹50,000. The settlement is then conducted directly with the advisor on a personal basis, who charges only 40% to 50% of the total amount, distributing the remainder among everyone involved in the scheme, including sometimes the general manager. Another unethical activity involves the body shop advisor offering to expedite claim approvals for additional parts in exchange for money or charging a lower amount on a personal basis when 2 or 3 panels get rejected and the customer is willing to get those repaired as well. Other fraudulent practices may mirror those seen in third-party workshops. Feedback holds significant importance for every advisor, and some may subtly influence it. For instance, they may inform customers that giving a 1-star rating will result in multiple calls from the CRE team to inquire about the issues. Therefore, customers who wish to avoid unnecessary calls may refrain from giving a 1-star rating. As I mentioned, there are numerous departments within a workshop. Do you know who the most liked person in the entire workshop is? It's the person who serves tea, as all the staff is divided by departments but united by chai, served twice a day. An authorised workshop has several revenue streams, including insurance, AMC, EW, parts, labour, body shop, scrapping parts, accessories, cleaning kits, tires, batteries, wheel alignment, and balancing. 3M also has a successful tie-up with many principal companies, where they not only supply their solutions but also oversee the polishing department by appointing their employees in the dealership. The government has lately shown interest in nullifying the rule that a warranty becomes void upon servicing the car at a third-party garage. However, is it really possible without having a proper data infrastructure to track those repairs conducted outside the authorised workshop? And most importantly, how will it become a win-win situation for the dealer?

Plastic bag

In the research I conducted, I asked various vendors about their plastic carry bag sales. Yes, plastic bags! We were so used to getting home items that wouldn't fit in our pockets in a plastic bag that we rarely went out with a reusable one, often without a shopping plan. Plastic bags were also given away for free for years until the Indian government banned single-use plastic items, including plastic bags and straws below 120 microns, in 2022. Many people thought about how hard and inconvenient it would be to adapt to a life without receiving items like vada pav, groceries, hardware, and food in plastic carry bags, as well as without plastic straws. This ban led to significant changes in how Indian consumers shopped. Let me explain what businesses did: Some switched to paper bags, which were free but inconvenient and less durable. Others continued to provide plastic bags illegally until they were fined a hefty ₹5,000 as first-time offenders. Some offered approved bags for free, while many opted for 125-micron plastic bags but started charging for them, ranging from ₹5 to ₹50 depending on the size. Now, the same consumer who couldn't imagine shopping without a plastic bag a few days ago starts carrying a bag with them when they go out with planned purchases. Some even manage with paper bags, use their pockets, utilize their vehicle's boot, or try to fit everything in their own bag instead of buying a separate one for each item or vendor. So you see, a simple thing like a plastic bag, which people instantly saw the benefit of using, was replaced by numerous alternatives as people chose to save ₹5 over convenience. Typically, people don't have time to invest in understanding entirely new things that require too much effort unless they realise the instant benefit. For example, if I tell you I own a gym, you can instantly grasp the benefit of subscribing and have a fair idea of what you're signing up for without me having to explain further. This illustrates how "Jugaad" is deeply ingrained in our culture. While some still prioritise convenience over cashback, the trend is shifting, especially among millennials, who are becoming more conscious of their choices. Take, for instance, Khidki Vada, one of Kalyan's oldest and most renowned vada pav shops, serving around 200 customers daily since 1967. Previously, they provided 200 plastic bags daily, but now they only distribute 10 plastic bags among the same 200 customers, marking a significant 95% decrease. Similar trends are observed at other establishments like Dmart, Reliance Smart, wine shops, and restaurants in Kalyan. These places cater to the majority of the population, which is the primary target audience for startups aiming to serve the top 100 million or lower-income segments. These individuals typically own, or aspire to own, a car on average.

Here's another example: At petrol pumps during peak hours, two-wheeler riders typically wait around 12 minutes. However, there's always one queue that appears much faster, with an estimated wait time of just 6 minutes. Wondering why? It's because this queue offers premium-quality petrol for an additional ₹5 per liter. Despite the longer wait, many opt for this queue, valuing their time differently. Some only realize the price difference when it's their turn, leading to some dissatisfaction, but they still choose it. So, if an extra ₹5 is added and consumers find a way to avoid it, you must be clever about pricing, unit economics, and monetization, especially when aiming for innovation and scalability.

Thank you :)

Thank you for taking the time to read my book. Composed from my extensive notes, I'm pleasantly surprised at how quickly this book came together. With the aid of digital tools, I was able to complete the entire process from writing, editing and manuscript preparation to book cover design in less than 60 hours.

Your thoughts and feedback are invaluable to me. If you see areas for improvement, come across any inaccuracies, or simply wish to share your reading experience, I would be delighted to hear from you. Please feel free to reach out via email at pistolshrimp444@gmail.com or find me on all social media platforms using @sanmitdixit. I look forward to engaging with you.